BUCKLE UP AND ENJOY THE RIDE

BUCKLE UP AND ENJOY THE RIDE

FINDING YOUR OWN PATH TO RESILIENCE, GRATITUDE, AND PEACE

BILL CARR

Forbes | Books

Published by Forbes Books, Charleston, South Carolina.
An imprint of Advantage Media Group.

Printed in the United States of America.

10 9 8 7 6 5 4 3 2 1

ISBN: 979-8-88750-398-1 (Hardcover)
ISBN: 979-8-88750-399-8 (eBook)

Library of Congress Control Number: 2025907961

Cover design by Matthew Morse.
Layout design by Ruthie Wood.

06-02-2025 11:42

To all of us who seek a better path forward.

CONTENTS

IN APPRECIATION

I wish to express my gratitude to two remarkable women who continue, day by day, to help me become a better person:

- My stepmom, Mary Jo, whom I call "Mom," who's been a guiding light for me for over fifty-five years.
- My wife, Breeda, who likewise keeps me grounded—but has only had to do it for the last eighteen years. Guess she got the better end of that deal!

Others are gone but not forgotten:

- My mother, Celeste, who passed when I was fifteen. I share her heart.
- My grandmother, Edith, whom everyone called "Ma"—always there with her optimistic spirit.
- My many other moms—the mothers of my friends—who made me feel part of their families. When each of them passed, I felt as if I were losing my own mother all over again. My pain was love. These fine women include Mrs. Huff, who kept a plate set at dinnertime for me. Mrs. Keogh, who invited me over for game nights. Mrs. Streb, whose basement was a refuge for all sorts of activities. Mrs. DePyssler, who always made me feel at home. And Mrs. O'Malley, who was legally

blind but knew it was me as soon as I walked in the front door—*how did she do that?*

Other lights in my life, all good people with good souls:

- The two daughters and son that I brought to our marriage: Jennifer, Jeff, and Claire.
- The two sons and daughter that Breeda brought to our marriage: Anthony, Matt, and Jessica.
- The dear daughter we formally adopted as an adult: Nicole.

I would also like to acknowledge all the people who let me tell their stories in this book.

My appreciation, as well, to the staff at Forbes Books for shepherding me along the way, especially Bob Sheasley, who for two years has helped me write this book. As we shared stories, our voices became one, as if our souls merged.

To all who made this book possible, I am deeply grateful.

FOREWORD

BY RICHARD WALKER

The rain was coming in sideways on the day I met up with Bill Carr in Scotland for a round of golf. He and his son, Jeff, showed up in their rainsuits and proper waterproof golf shoes. Then my brother, Johnny, arrived for our foursome—in rugby shorts and tennis shoes. Johnny was a professional rugby player but only played golf a couple of times a year.

Bill teed up first and proceeded to hit his ball straight right, into the rough. Jeff snap-hooked his ball straight left, and my ball almost didn't find the planet! Johnny's turn. He stepped to the tee—no practice swings, no warm-up—and striped a 300-yard drive straight down the middle.

Bill stared at his club, then at Johnny, then back at his club, which he tossed in the air. "That's stinkin' garbage!" he said, or words to that effect. His language was a bit more colorful.

And that's Bill. He was poking fun at himself while making Johnny feel like a champ. That's his way, and I have seen it time and again. He lifts other people up, puts them at ease, and keeps everyone in good humor, and he's willing to do it at his own expense.

Golf is a passion we share, but we have been close friends and colleagues for nearly three decades. Several years ago, Bill handed me the reins to the company he founded—York Solutions—and it was there, by his words and example, that he taught me and all of us what it means to be a strong leader. I know Bill to be the most composed, thoughtful, and steady person I've ever met. No matter the circumstances, he never gets too high or too low.

Some relationships take time to build. Others are spontaneous, and that's how it was with Bill back in 1997, when a mutual business acquaintance suggested we meet. We hit it off in our first conversation, and not just because he showed up wearing a golf tie, though it helped. We talked about golf, and about business, but mostly we talked about life. I told my wife that night, "I don't know what's going to happen, but something good is going to come from meeting this guy."

Bill Carr isn't a typical leader. He leads quietly and effectively from the back, out of the limelight. He's like those alpha wolves who protect their pack from the rear. That's where you'll find Bill: making sure nobody gets left behind. Though he can step quickly to the front when necessary, he aims to empower others to lead. His priority was to maintain a welcoming workplace. When I became CEO, I asked him to tell me three things I should do to ensure success. "One, don't screw up the culture," he said. "Two, don't screw up the culture. And three? Don't screw up the culture."

During the 2008 financial crisis, I saw Bill's brand of leadership in action. I felt like throwing in the towel. As the market worsened, I figured I'd soon be going back to bricklaying again, which I used to do as a young man in Yorkshire. Bill stayed calm, focused, and optimistic.

After things turned around, he wrote me a heartfelt letter of gratitude, which I cherish to this day.

Again, that's Bill. He makes you feel like you're the one steering the ship. He doesn't tell you what to do. Instead, he asks questions to guide you: *Have you considered this? What if you tried that?* Through the years, Bill taught me how to focus on what really matters. When the pandemic hit, I found myself wondering: *What would Bill do?*

This book is sampling from Bill's journals through the years. He has collected a lifetime of stories, lessons, and hard-earned wisdom. I hear his voice on every page—humble, thoughtful, wisecracking, warmhearted, and always a bit self-deprecating. If you're like me, you also will see something of yourself on every page, as his stories lead you to reflect on your own. This book isn't just about Bill. It's about all of us.

In these essays, you'll see Bill as a teenager promising his dying mother he'd look after his siblings. You'll read about the time he stood over his newborn daughter's crib, overwhelmed by how much of life is beyond our control. You'll be with him in Vietnam as he tells you about the day when he grew up there. You'll hear him explain why he quit college just short of a doctorate in chemistry and went after an entirely different career. All that and a lot more.

My friend Bill doesn't pretend to have all the answers. What he does have is a quiet strength that comes from years of facing life's messiness head-on. He's still learning, still smiling—and still throwing golf clubs.

INTRODUCTION

BUCKLE UP, ENJOY THE RIDE!

Let's take a long ride together now, to places familiar and places unknown. I want to tell you some stories. On these pages is an account of life as I've known it, for better and for worse. I am seventy-four years old as I write these words, and the road I've traveled has taken many turns. Along the way, I've figured out a thing or two.

You have your own stories: different from mine but in some ways the same. Whatever road you took, I am sure that you, like me, have experienced sudden sharp curves and unexpected detours. You have probably run out of gas a few times and come to some dead ends. The scenery at times has been dreary but so often beautiful.

Let's slow down now to compare notes. My hope is that as I tell you my stories you will reflect on your own experiences. In that way, this book isn't so much about me as it is about you. I want to stir up your memories. I want my stories to be a catalyst for your retrospection. That's why I've included blank pages at the end of each essay in this book.

As you read about how I have navigated life, consider your own choices—which would you repeat, which would you change? What wisdom would you impart to your children, or to a friend encountering challenges not unlike the ones that you have faced? What guidance do you wish you had received?

I'm not suggesting we dwell on what has happened to us, but we should learn from it. I have met so many people who get stuck in the past. They just keep replaying their regrets and mistakes and all the injustices they have endured. I have met others who are stuck another way: They replay their glory days, forgetting that celebrations are fleeting.

Fretting about the future is futile, too. So many variables can disrupt the best-laid plans. Yes, it's good to imagine a destination. You don't want to feel as if you're wandering aimlessly. Still, if you have faced detours and curves before, you can be sure they will come again—and try as you might, you won't know when. Tomorrow holds possibilities but not promises.

Our stories help us process the past, come to terms with it, accept it. We cannot rewrite it, any more than we can dictate the future. Once we accept those truths, we gain the resilience to live for today. Think about it—where else but the present should you be living? Today is when you can appreciate the sunsets and hear the laughter and dry the tears. Free from the burden of yesterday and tomorrow, you can have a good day—no matter what has happened, no matter what is yet to be.

Let's get started. I invite you now to come along with me. No need to go it alone. All of us are on this journey together—and so, as you will hear me say more than once in these essays: Buckle up, and enjoy the ride!

Who, then, is Bill Carr? I'm a product of the South Side of Chicago, as you will see in the pages ahead. I did my share of stupid things as a kid, and maybe a few sensible ones. I quit college after screwing around for a year, just in time to lose the draft lottery and land in Vietnam—which is where I grew up and decided to make something of myself.

I chose chemistry for my college major just to prove to myself that I could master something that seemed exceedingly difficult. A summer job evolved into a lucrative career, and in time I found myself at the helm of my own IT services business, York Solutions, based in Chicago and the Twin Cities area.

Some of my stories that lie ahead are about growing up during my South Side days. Others are about what I have learned from family and friends and colleagues. We learn best from those we know well, and the life lessons sink in when we hear them as narratives.

That is why this book has so many stories. Memories do not come neatly packaged. One moment our thoughts go to yesterday and the next to yesteryear. Therefore, you will find no particular timeline in this book. You could just as well start reading it in the middle, or from back to front. Though each of the essays in this book could stand alone, I have organized them loosely into three sections. The themes, essentially, are these:

1. Life is arbitrary. It's a crapshoot.
2. You can make the most of it. You can find your own way.
3. It's all worthwhile. There are gifts you can give yourself.

If you're like me, you'll see that much of what we experience seems like a series of random events with unintended consequences. Much of what happens to us is beyond our control. What is within our control is how we respond to all the twists and turns and unknowns of life.

The trick, I have learned, is knowing what we can influence and what we should just let be. We can't do anything about the cards we're dealt. We're at the mercy of the shuffle. We can only play the hand we get as best we can—and that's what makes all the difference. That's how we can find our own way.

I hope that as you reflect on your own stories, you will feel encouraged to look at life a little differently—not with complaints or regrets about what happened to you, but instead with gratitude, forgiveness, and a desire to reach out to help others, to lead by example. Together we can do what we can to make our lives, and the lives of those around us, a little better.

SECTION ONE

WELCOME TO THE CRAPSHOOT

Life is a roll of the dice. We are born into a world that seems indifferent to us. We don't get to choose how we start out, nor much of what happens to us. Will we be born into wealth or poverty? Into a time of peace or war? To parents who hug us or who ignore us? Nor can we predict or influence much of what happens to us. In this section, we look at what it means to live with the truth that the only certainty is that nothing is certain.

In **"Claire in the Crib,"** I reflect on a day when I picked up my newborn daughter at day care. What would become of her and the other little ones in that room as life happened to them? They didn't know what they didn't know—and in a way, I could take comfort in their innocence.

"Life is Not a Straight Line" looks at how life's zigs and zags, as scary as they can be, force us to adapt. As we deal with unexpected challenges, we have the opportunity for growth.

"A Series of Unintended Consequences" explores how our decisions lead to outcomes we might never have anticipated and take us to places we might never have gone.

"The Zip Code Lottery" considers how where we're born can shape our chances in life. Growing up on the South Side of Chicago, I saw firsthand the economic and racial divides within my city. I got lucky. Others didn't.

"One Size Does Not Fit All" was a lesson I learned as I took unconventional paths: from my childhood, to Vietnam, to quitting college just short of a doctorate. Life tries to force us into a mold—but we can find success in unexpected places and on our own terms.

"Defeat Is When You Give Up," not when life knocks you down. Here, I reflect on my son Jeff's fight to overcome addiction. As a parent, I struggled, too—but I didn't give up on him, even when I had no answers. More importantly, he didn't give up on himself.

"Success or Failure? All in How You Look at It": We can think of life as a continuum with high and low points. What we call victories and defeats are fleeting moments. It's how we live along the way that counts.

CLAIRE IN THE CRIB

I opened the door, and there was Claire, my newborn daughter, lying in a crib at the day care center. Several other cribs lined the walls of the crowded room. I stepped to her side. She shifted in her slumber, her tiny fists clenched.

I looked around the room, where staff workers leaned over the cribs, offering bottles and soothing words. The infants were clothed in pinks and blues. Some were white babies, some Black, some Hispanic. Each born innocent and oblivious to the world awaiting them. They lived entirely in the moment, wanting only their bottles and someone to cuddle them.

One of the babies began to cry. I felt, as I stood there, a wave of sadness. I wanted to cry, too.

At age forty-seven, I had become a dad for the third time. My marriage of fifteen years had long since ended in divorce, and I had started dating again. One day, my girlfriend of several years knocked on my door. "Guess what? I'm pregnant," she said. We had just broken up.

The ensuing weeks were rough. She would have this baby or not—but I had no say in the matter. I had no control. She chose to become a mom, and her decision came as a relief. I could see a path forward again. It was the not knowing that was most disconcerting. We resolved to stay close during the pregnancy and to work together in raising the child. We would never become a married couple, but together we would be loving parents. Claire is now twenty-seven and has always been incredibly close to both of us.

Claire's mom was a nurse and successful in her career. She stayed home with her baby daughter for several months but soon had to return to her professional duties. Her rotating shifts and overtime meant that Claire was with me a lot of the time. Even when she wasn't, I had to be prepared to drop everything and pick her up at the day care if her mom couldn't leave work.

You may recall the movie *Three Men and a Baby*. This was only one man and a baby! I wasn't stressed-out, though. I felt confident in what I was doing because I had been through it twice before. Also in my household at the time were my daughter Jennifer, who had been out of the crib for twenty years, and my son Jeff, who was sixteen. They were around the house much of the time, available to be big sister and brother for Claire.

Those were some of the best days of my life. Unique, certainly. I got to watch all the old Disney movies again. Seeing them through Claire's eyes, they actually seemed really good. If Claire misbehaved, I set the microwave timer to count down her time-out—and it got so that I needed only to point at the microwave for her to get her act together.

One evening, after picking her up at day care, we sat together on the back-porch staircase: me with a bottle of cold beer, she with her sippy cup. I looked over at her, smiling. She was older now, jabbering away about the things that matter to little girls. For now, Claire was the picture of innocence. I knew that as the years passed, she would be heading out into a world that wasn't always kind. A big girl's tears would come, and one day I would not be there to dry them.

I thought again about that afternoon visit to the day care when I had felt such sorrow. Such a setting should bring only joy. What had bothered me? I had imagined all those babies in that room not as they were but as they might become. For that moment, they all were the same soft bundles, smelling (at best) of soap and Similac. They were pure—but life would happen. They would win or lose, rise or fall, and much—if not all of it—would be through no choice of their own.

Community leaders? Inmates? Long life, short life, healthy or hurting—who knew? Some would flourish, some would struggle, some might even perish. At some point, each would lie awake staring at the ceiling, long past midnight. They would experience the assortment of joys and sadnesses common to humanity. How would my own little Claire, lying there in the crib, turn out once the world had its random way with her? Who and what would cross her path, and when, and why? I could not see the path forward—and, again, it was the not knowing that troubled me.

"Will you draw a picture with me, Daddy?" Claire's request awoke me from my troubled thoughts. She was on the floor now, hovering over a coloring book, scribbling randomly, her big box of crayons spilling around her.

As a good dad, I started to tell her she must keep within the lines. "Here's how you do it, Claire," I began, bending down to show her the proper way, but then I stopped. Why should she have to stay within the lines? She was only three, and I was asking her to conform to our adult world, filled with lines we must never cross. We admonish one another to grow up and not be childish—to which I say, "What's the rush?" Life will come soon enough.

I smiled at Claire again and sat with her on the floor. She was the center, for now, of her own world, an innocent and carefree one.

She didn't know what she didn't know. All too soon she would be discovering what it supposedly means to be all grown-up.

"Sure, Claire, I'll draw with you. Let's make a picture of *you*!" I said. Giggling, she held out her big box of choices—and I reached for the brightest colors.

BEFORE LIFE HAPPENS

Touched by an Angel was a popular TV show back in 1997, the year Claire was born. One episode has stayed with me through the years. I have thought about it while raising all my children through to adulthood. And, as I watch my grandchildren at play, I think about it still.

In the episode, a little girl named Melissa has been hearing voices. Her parents consult a psychologist who suggests a variety of things that don't work. Finally, an angel named Tess sits down with the parents to tell them what is going on. It's good news and bad news. The good news is Melissa will soon stop hearing the voices. And the bad news: She will soon stop hearing the voices.

Tess explains to the concerned parents that before babies are born, they are with the angels, and they can still hear them awhile after birth. Melissa, in her innocence, has heard them longer than most. Soon, that innocence will be ending–and she will only hear the world's noise.

I saw that episode before Claire was born. How long would her innocence last? I was already mourning its passing. I wanted her to grow up, of course—but how fast? She and all my children have long since grown up to deal with life in their own ways, but it still saddens me to know the voices must fade as life happens.

I watch my grandchildren today at play, rolling around together. They laugh and then argue, and within minutes they're laughing again, together and inseparable. Life will pull them in different directions. It is inevitable. The world is waiting for them, and they will take their place in it, whatever that might be. Too soon they will have to grow up and move out into the world, where the angel voices have grown silent.

For now, at least, I am grateful that they can just keep on rolling. I find the openness and honesty of children to be refreshing. They tend to do a better job than adults at letting you know what they are feeling, what they need, what they want. That comes from the innocence they have yet to lose.

I hear parents yelling at their children: "Don't act so childish!" Or a tough-guy dad will warn his crying little boy: "Be a man!" Really? How's he supposed to do that? We shouldn't hurry our kids along to adulthood. They'll get there too soon as it is, only to discover the truth: Adults are just screwed-up children.

THOUGHTS:

LIFE IS NOT A STRAIGHT LINE

We all struggle with the tough times we go through in life. *What did I do to deserve this?* we wonder. *When will it all be over?* If you believe in God, you may have one big question for him: *Why?*

Humans are not meant to live their lives in straight lines. Straight lines provide no diversity, no challenge, no new ideas, and no change—and without change, how can we have growth?

Change is pretty scary, isn't it? Anybody who gets married must be concerned, at some level, about being committed to another person for life, considering that more than half of marriages fail. You're deluding yourself if you think you know how your life will be after having a child. Who has ever left a job and moved out of state, away from family and friends, without being a little freaked-out? Or if you are jobless and can't pay your bills, how can you not feel like a failure?

Remember, life is not a straight line.

Several years ago, I went to an addiction meeting as a parent of a struggling son. My son went to a separate breakout session, where a visitor who had himself once been an addict offered some compelling advice. "How do you know when you've hit rock bottom?" he asked. "It's when you stop digging." My son told me he had realized, upon hearing those words, that he had been digging a hole most of his adult life. It wouldn't be easy, he said, but he knew he needed to stop digging and start building his life.

How would it turn out? He had no idea. Sometimes in life, you just get what you get.

What is interesting about life is you find out more about yourself during the tough times when life does a zig or a zag on you. This is when your brain starts developing new pathways and expanding its horizons. If you have ever tried to learn a language or a new musical instrument as an adult, you know exactly what I mean.

I recently read about an Alzheimer's disease study that followed several hundred nuns for decades, starting in 1986. Conducted by epidemiologist David Snowdon and funded by the National Institute on Aging, the study focused on nuns so that it could control variables such as drug and alcohol use, housing, and reproductive history. The nuns kept detailed journals, and regular testing recorded their cognitive state. Many died in their eighties and nineties and had agreed to donate brain tissue for research. In some of the tissues, the researchers detected plaque associated with dementia—but the nuns had exhibited no symptoms. The study found that lifestyle and education had contributed to the lack of symptoms, particularly among the nuns with the most articulate and positive journals. Their brains had developed neuron circuits to override the pathways affected by the plaque.

If our brains can find a way around obstacles, so can we.

We will all face incredible challenges along the way. If you have been around awhile, you already have. A few years ago, a survey asked people what age they considered to be their happiest. You might think it was in their teens or early twenties, before life got complicated. No, the happiest people were in their eighties. They had been through life's uncertainties and surprises. They had learned, adapted, and adjusted. They were at peace.

A good, fulfilled, happy life is full of twists and turns. You will face all sorts of crap you wish you didn't have to deal with—but once you stop digging, you can start building. The tough times will yield to growth, confidence, wisdom, and peace, hopefully before you are in your eighties.

Remember, life is not meant to be a straight line. So buckle up, and enjoy the ride.

THOUGHTS:

A SERIES OF UNINTENDED CONSEQUENCES

Whenever I tell my stepmom about the misfortunes of others, she reminds me that God has a plan for each of us. I'm seventy-four years old as I write this, and I still don't know God's plan. In my time, I have seen a lot of bad get piled on good people, while plenty of good happens to bad people.

I can only conclude that God puts us here with free will, then he lets us do our thing as life happens to us, and then he takes us back. I can't explain what happens in between. I'm just sorry he has to watch the mess we have created on earth.

We mortals can plan all we want, but to what end? So much is random. If you are married, consider how you met your spouse. You might say it was destiny, but most likely it was happenstance. You encountered someone—in a bar, on the job, on vacation—who just happened to be there when you were there, the stranger across a crowded room. What if that coworker had taken a different job, or you had missed your flight to Cancun, or you had departed the tavern just as your future spouse was entering? Would you ever have met?

If you think about the other relationships in your life beyond your immediate family, they are probably also the result of chance.

In my business life, I often tried to project how the company and our stock would look in five or ten years. We either missed those goals or surpassed them. I now know that you *can't* know. Too many variables. Who can predict when the economy will be good or bad? The best employees don't always stick around. Nor do the best clients. You can only make an educated guess and then keep your fingers crossed.

I am reluctant to spend too much time setting goals. I try to focus on the only things I can truly control—my attitude and how I treat people. Eventually, those two things have more impact on future results than goal-setting ever will. Through the years, I have learned to take it as it comes—and to try, as best I know how, to protect myself from the downside.

That's the approach advocated by Nassim Nicholas Taleb in his 2012 book *Antifragile: Things That Gain from Disorder* and other works. In short, Taleb says this: In a world we do not understand, we can gain from disruptions and uncertainties if we make ourselves less vulnerable to risk. If we don't let mistakes bury us, we can learn and grow from them.

A simple example among many complex ones: If you have a business appointment at nine o'clock in the morning, plan to be there at eight thirty. If traffic is light, you get there half an hour early and can put that time to good use. You could review your notes and prepare for the meeting. You could listen to music. You could call a friend or one of your kids. If traffic is heavy, you still get there a few minutes early. Not only have you protected yourself from the disruption, you could even gain from it. The uncertainty of the traffic cannot hurt you and could even help you.

We all face such disruptions and risks. To deal with them, we can take our cue from the way investors hedge against the downside using calculated precautions. In many areas of life, we can "invest" in the things that shield us from harm—and that's a pretty good dividend.

Here's an example we all know: using your seatbelt. Investing a few seconds of your time could save your life. When I was in my twenties, I was speeding along in a convertible one day when I lost control. The car flipped over, and I wasn't wearing a seatbelt. Neither was my passenger. We escaped with our lives only because the car rolled over so fast that centrifugal force kept us in our seats. I'm lucky to be alive to tell this story. Rest assured, from that point on, I invested the few seconds to buckle up.

A few years ago, while refurbishing a house, I fell down a staircase. With a glass of wine in my hand, I tripped on the top step—and there was no handrail. I hit the floor hard, tearing my rotator cuff and damaging four vertebrae. With physical therapy, I recovered. Once again, I saw how easily life's downsides can surprise you—and how easily I could have invested in prevention. I should have installed a handrail before letting anyone, particularly me, use those stairs.

When you buy car or homeowner's insurance, you're protecting yourself from the downside. You hope you'll never need that policy, but if you do, you'll be glad you invested in it. Likewise, the simple steps we can take to safeguard ourselves or our property can save us from catastrophic consequences. You can't count on luck.

In other words, life is not a straight line. Expect the twists and turns. They will be sure to come. Of that, at least, you can be certain. Things just happen, but that doesn't mean we should shrug and give up. We must deal with them. What seems like a setback we can turn to good, if we don't give in to despair. It's our job to figure out how to get from beginning to end.

My stepmom tells me that turning the bad into good is what God can do for us. She lives in Indianapolis now and is well into her nineties. When we get together, we have long talks about such matters. I take a look around, and I don't get it. I do see plenty that's just fine, but if I give God credit for the good, I'd have to blame him for the bad, and I'm just not going there.

Dealing with the uncertainty of life is complicated. Who's to say what decision is exactly right or wrong?

What seems to be a good solution can turn out to be bad and vice versa. "It's complicated," as a therapist would say. That's what you probably will have heard if you have ever been to personal counseling. You share a dilemma, such as, "My daughter says I should pay all her rent or she'll get kicked out and live on the street. What should I do?" And the therapist nods, jots down a note, and tells you there's a lot that goes into such a decision. That means there's no easy answer. If you give her the rent money, you might be giving her the break she needs. Or you might be paying for her next trip to the casino.

We all encounter similar situations in life. So much depends on the people and circumstances. Trained professionals can give educated and helpful advice and help you think things through, but they don't pretend to have all the answers because there are none. There are too many variables. Life is a series of unintended consequences.

I consider myself fortunate. I have had my portion of bad things and some extraordinarily tough times, but I don't have bad days. I wake up each morning. I have family and friends and a passion to pursue what interests me. Still, I am no happier today just because things are going well. For any of us, new troubles can be just around the corner. No need to ask why. No need to give up. You can face them, and you will survive, often for the better.

THOUGHTS:

THE ZIP CODE LOTTERY

One summer evening, when I was seventeen years old and walking home from work, a group of Black guys surrounded me in front of my high school. One of them was on crutches, with his leg in a cast, and he hobbled up close to me. "Your money, man," he shouted as his friends circled me. "Now!"

No way was I going to hand over my wallet. My week's paycheck was in it! It didn't occur to me that they wouldn't be able to cash it anyway. I dug into my pocket and pulled out some quarters and dimes. "S'all I got, really," I said.

My generosity somehow did not impress them. A moment later, I was on the ground, my arms around my head, as the guy with the broken leg beat me with his crutch. His friends found this to be hilarious. After a while, they got tired of the entertainment and left me alone.

Fast-forward several weeks. The coat-check girl at the restaurant where I worked full-time as a busboy told me she was going to a dance that evening at her Catholic school. "Maybe I'll see you there," she said with a smile. I took the hint.

Her school wasn't in my parish. In Chicago, it's all about parishes—and though I was Catholic, I went to public school. I looked for her that night in the crowded gymnasium. I asked a few kids if anyone knew her and had seen her. No dice. So, I left.

Out on the sidewalk, a group of white guys surrounded me—and one of them was on crutches, his leg in a cast. He hobbled up to me. "What're you doing here?" he demanded. He looked me up and down, sneering as if I stunk of public school. "You don't belong here. You're not one of us." His friends started pushing me.

I stammered out the names of some of my Catholic friends, all from my own parish. "Never heard of them," the guy with the broken leg said—and a moment later, I was on the ground, my arms around my head, as he beat me with his crutch. They all laughed till they got tired of tormenting me, and then I was able to scramble away.

And so, as a teenager, I learned a lesson that I carry with me to this day. Beware of people on crutches. They do not mean you well. And never, ever trust anyone with a broken leg. I've become prejudiced that way, I confess.

There's a lesson there somewhere. Through the years, I've often reflected on what I learned during those late summer days of the late '60s. You might say I got some sense beaten into me. Prejudice isn't as simple as black and white. But it does have a whole lot to do with brokenness.

I grew up on the South Side of Chicago, which has a reputation for being a hotbed for crime. That's the way it is in some zip codes there, but not in Beverly. It's a neighborhood of quiet, tree-lined streets and handsome brick homes on the far south. It's part of the city but has a suburban feel. We lived in a nice big house a few blocks from the train tracks that took you downtown. Many of the people living there were affluent professionals—doctors, lawyers, accountants. Everybody knew everybody, it seemed. Many of the families were Irish Catholic or Italian. The woman in the house behind us had twelve kids. In that neighborhood, our five-kid family was a small one.

My father, Bill, had been a "tinman" who sold aluminum siding in Springfield before getting a job in Chicago as a chemical sales engineer. No way could he have afforded our house on a salary of $6,000 a year and with a family of five kids. I'm sure my grandfather helped foot the bills.

My parents struggled financially. I suppose I should have been aware of that. The signs were clearly there. We drank powdered milk and Tang. Dinner was often a mystery meat that my parents optimistically called "steak," served with a side of instant mashed potatoes. My old clothes got handed down to my brother.

Such was our life there in our enclave of zip code 60643. We were a lower-middle-class family living in an upper-middle-class community. I was privileged to go to good schools. I was lucky. I won the zip code lottery.

The neighborhood was all white back then, but my high school was integrated. When school let out, the Black kids headed east, and the white kids headed west. It was rumored that a Black kid could be admitted only after two white kids had been admitted. The Beverly community organization hoped to do something to prevent white flight. To fend off "blockbusting," it discouraged homeowners from putting out for-sale signs. Most home sales were negotiated at cocktail parties. God forbid that a Black family see a sign and call a realtor and decide to move in. *There goes the neighborhood.*

When my parents moved to Beverly in 1956, the neighbor next door was a Jewish doctor who was the city's health commissioner. He and his daughters kept the house in immaculate shape. He eventually sold the place to a white family from Tennessee. They couldn't afford to take care of the place, and it showed in the peeling paint and broken-down cars in the driveway. By the late 1960s, the house had been sold again, this time to a Black family who owned a bus company. They cleaned up the mess, and the house was soon immaculate once again.

So much for blockbusting. This was block-*building*, but a lot of folks didn't see it that way. What they saw were Black faces increasingly coming to their beautiful town. Black faces, like the ones in those other zip codes not so far away, which they saw as desolate places of crime and poverty, where drug dealers prowled the streets. The attitude was clear: *Those people don't belong here. They're not like us. Why would anyone want to live that way?*

If they had stopped to think about it, maybe they would have recognized that crime and poverty were the real problem. We should all hate economic injustice, but we shouldn't hate its victims. "Those people" are just people—and they didn't choose to live that way, any more than they chose the pigmentation of their skin.

Prejudices are preconceived notions, and those aren't always bad. Our experiences inform us. That's why we don't touch a hot stove—we prejudge that the result will be pain and blisters. Prejudging can help us navigate a complicated world. The trouble is that prejudice is often based on faulty perceptions. We must put them to the test. On what were they founded?

At dinner recently, my brother Steve and I started talking about the urban phenomenon of flash mobs, where packs of urban youths, sometimes by the hundreds, go on a looting spree. My brother rolled his eyes, disgusted. Even a generally progressive type like Steve has his limits, and he felt nothing resembling tolerance for such lawlessness. He suggested some rather harsh remedies.

"No question about it, it's awful," I said, "but think about this: If you were born where a lot of them were born, and raised like they were, would you be any different? If we had grown up in one of those zip codes filled with poverty and drugs and crime and racism, how would we be?"

"I'd make different decisions," Steve said, flatly

"Sure, we'd all like to think that," I told him. "But how do you know? Is it really that easy for people to reinvent themselves?"

I admire my brother's faith in the human power to choose right over wrong. It just all seems too simple. How can we expect that people who grew up in hell will suddenly have an epiphany and make enlightened choices? Sure, sometimes they do. You hear a lot of stories about them. You don't hear about those whose environment seals their destiny forever. We celebrate the few who break free. We ignore the many who stay trapped in their misery.

The best predictor of wealth is a zip code. The US Census for 2020 found a nationwide median income of $45,870 for Black households and $71,231 for white households. Break that down into the wealthiest and the poorest zip codes, and the racial disparity is clear. So is the despair. It cuts lives short. Zip codes only a few miles apart can differ by decades in life expectancy, according to statistics from the CDC. Life expectancy tends to be lowest in the zip codes for Black neighborhoods.

In 2019, residents of Chicago's affluent Streeterville neighborhood (zip code 60611) lived to be ninety, on average, while nine miles away, in the poor South Side neighborhood of Englewood (zip code 60621), the typical life expectancy was sixty. That thirty-year gap was the nation's largest. Englewood's median household income was $30,163 in 2022, according to census statistics. For Streeterville, it was $126,812.

Statistics like that make it pretty clear what's going on. And yet we so often hear the angry refrain: *What is* wrong *with those people?* Far better to ask what *happened* to them—because a million things could influence how life turns out. We are so quick to judge people who had no control over where they were born and how they were raised. Nobody can agree on solutions to our society's ills. More prisons?

Drug rehab centers? Food and rent subsidies? Those are treatments but far from cures. We need to dig deeper into rooting out the causes. Any real change would take at least two decades—from the time kids are born until they are into their twenties. Our politicians, elected for two or four years, aren't likely to look for real answers.

Nobel Prize–winner James Heckman, a University of Chicago economist, has conducted extensive research showing that effective childcare can pay great dividends, not only for the child later in life but also for our society. A nurturing mother, in particular, no doubt plays a major role in how a child turns out, yet researchers haven't examined the nature of that impact, Heckman said in an interview hosted by the American Enterprise Institute. "Nobody wants to talk about the family," he added, "and the family's the whole story. And it's the whole story about a lot of social and economic issues."

So many factors can determine the kind of path that kids take as they grow up. It can be as simple as whether anyone cares to hug them. A warm touch works wonders. It rewires the brain.

I've often considered what early experiences contributed to the wiring of my own brain. In my time, I've made some bad decisions along with the good ones—but I take zero credit for anything that worked out well. Much of what made me who I am wasn't a matter of choice. It was random. Still, I learned plenty from the people in my life and the situations I encountered. It wasn't just the zip code lottery that I won. I lucked out in the family lottery, too.

I was the oldest of five kids—four boys and a girl. My mom, Celeste, was the embodiment of kindness, always warmhearted and affectionate. My dad's job required him to travel often, so in his absence, I was the closest thing to an adult in the family—and that's how my mom talked to me, even when I was only seven or eight. When I think of her, I conjure this snapshot from my long-ago boyhood: I am lying on the porch glider, my head in her lap, and she is cleaning my ears with a bobby pin, as mothers did in those days. Even today, recalling those moments of her gentle warmth, I drift away.

In 1963, when I was thirteen years old, my mom developed cancer. She died when I was fifteen. Shortly before she passed, on an evening when my parents had friends over for a party, I went to her bedside to check on her. She was weak from chemotherapy but started to whisper something. I closed the door to quiet the sounds of laughter from the party downstairs, and then leaned close to her. She looked deeply into my eyes.

"I want you to take care of your brothers and sister for me," she said. I saw a world of worries in her eyes, as vivid to me today as sixty years ago. I can only imagine how she felt, knowing she was leaving her young children behind.

"Will you do that, Willie? Will you look after your brothers and sister?" I told her I would. Her eyes softened, and she went back to sleep.

During those two years that my mom was sick, my grandmother on my father's side (known as Ma to all of us) stepped in to help. She had long been a big part of our lives. My mom didn't drive, so my grandmother would take us on outings to amusement parks, the Chicago beaches, museums, and more. She moved into our house to help her clueless son manage a household with five young kids. She was one of the most positive and optimistic people I've ever met.

With such fine women in one's life, who wouldn't feel they'd won the family lottery? I had another reason to feel that way, though. At age fifteen, with my mom gone and my father away so often, I found that I could do whatever I wanted, whenever I wanted. My dad required only that he not have to come to the principal's office or police station to get me out of trouble. I failed at both those requests.

I was thrilled to have such free rein over my life at such a young age. I got to experience the real world and figure out life along the way. During my first two years of high school, I worked evenings as a busboy pretty much full time, sometimes sixty hours a week. In my junior and senior years, I cleaned factory offices after school. I had money and a car. I got lots of dates with a lot of different girls. Life was good.

School was not going so well, however—at least academically. My grades were shaky. That was the downside to my newfound freedom. Socially, though, I did fine. I joined a fraternity at my high school, becoming its president in my junior and senior years and changing a lot of stupid rules. I was a member of my high school golf team, but they only played four on a team, and I was number five. That's right, I sucked at golf. No comment on how well I'm doing today.

In 1968, during my senior year, my dad remarried. His new bride also had five children, and, as in our family, it was four boys and a girl. I was my dad's best man at the wedding. My new stepsister was the maid of honor.

As I write these words, I look forward to my stepmom reading this book. She is ninety-four years old, and for over fifty-five years now she has been the strongest influence in my life. She has had her share of life's challenges. Through it all, she believes that God has a plan—and she is pleased to tell me that again almost every time we talk.

"I suppose I should stop preaching to you," she told me during one of our recent talks. I don't see it as preaching, though. I see it as great conversation with a woman who cares about me and has many years of wisdom to share. Whether I agree with her isn't the point. I admire the depth and conviction she brings to the table. Her spiritual nature is compelling. She challenges me to think, and who wouldn't appreciate that?

"No, don't stop, Mom," I told her. "Never stop."

Now you can see my trifecta. My warm and caring mother, who died too young at the age of thirty-eight. My relentlessly optimistic grandmother. My incredibly strong and deeply spiritual stepmom. Three marvelous women who contributed so much to the wiring of my brain. You don't always have much choice in the people who come into your life and help to make you who you are. Sometimes, like me, you just get lucky.

THOUGHTS:

ONE SIZE DOES NOT FIT ALL

The rules go like this: First, attend a top-notch high school. If your zip code doesn't have one, study hard anyway. Get good grades so that you still have a chance to get into a decent college, even if you have no idea how you will pay for it. Then, at age eighteen or so, boldly declare what you want to do for the rest of your life, and find the money to get a four-year degree in something related to it. Go to work for "the Man" at a big company. Start working your way up through the ranks. Get married and produce 1.9 kids. Buy a house in the 'burbs.

You know the story. It's a familiar pattern, from crib to coffin. The rules lay out the basics of what you should be doing, and when, and where. Countless people comply without considering why. They don't see themselves as getting put into a box. They see themselves as sensible, dutiful citizens, and most of them are.

That wasn't my path. I did luck out with a good zip code and high school, but I got mediocre grades, went to college by default, screwed around and quit, and then got drafted into a jungle. I woke up in time to go back to college the day after I came home, with just a couple hundred bucks in my pocket. I studied very hard. Just short of my doctorate, I chucked it all to try my hand at something unrelated to what I had expected to do for the rest of my life.

Even though my own path veered off the beaten one, I encouraged my kids to play by the rules as they headed into the world. We didn't talk much about whether to "follow your passion." Frankly, I didn't think about it much. The rules say to "do these things first"—and the passion follows, I suppose.

If you are like me, you don't have to look far to find plenty of folks, even among friends and family, who have made their own way in life by a different set of rules. These are all smart people—but a traditional, formal education wasn't their way, for whatever reason.

Maybe they tried out the classroom setting, but it didn't fit them. Perhaps they felt that it was a waste of their time to study hard when they had no clue what their career would be (and, as teenagers, precious few do). Instead, they kept in step to a different beat and marched off to find their own definition of success.

Or maybe college was out of the question, and they didn't get a chance to see whether it would be a good fit. Life got in the way. They spent long hours laboring at a job that fed their belly but not their spirit. Their passion, even if they were aware of one, would have to wait. Survival comes first—and dreams tend to fade as those checks keep rolling round.

Such souls didn't choose to be wired differently. Neither did they choose the circumstances into which they were born, nor the setbacks they experienced as life had its way with them. Still, they often feel judged. "Don't knock on my door looking for a job," says the Man, "if you don't have the papers to show you're any good." They feel pressure from family and friends to conform. Worst of all, they begin judging themselves. Sometimes, they feel like misfits because they cannot accommodate someone else's idea of success.

Though I have stepped down from the active leadership of my company, York Solutions, I've dedicated my career to helping those unconventional talents succeed. I am proud of the role York has played. We have reached out to people who feel stuck and need a helping hand—or sometimes just a word of encouragement—to move forward. We have found smart people with the right skills to fill positions at companies that need them. It hasn't always been easy, particularly during the Great Recession when even top IT executives were casting about for employment.

One of the newer programs, still in its early years as I write this, looks for IT talent in places other than among typical college graduates. The Barriers to Entry program was developed by Richard Walker, my successor as York Solutions' CEO, with the help of a dedicated and brilliant team. The program thoroughly tests applicants to see if they have the right stuff. The applicants do not need to show that they have the right education and training. Our company provides all that, at no cost. These applicants might know next to nothing about IT. Instead, they must demonstrate that they are hard-wired for excellence in the field, regardless of their current station in life. We find people with an inborn aptitude for complex technological concepts, and then we train them for placement at top companies in great need of their skills.

The Barriers to Entry program has discovered extraordinary IT talent in unlikely places—laboring in warehouses, stocking shelves at supermarkets, sweating in factories. They often have been struggling to put food on the table for their families. Others are doing OK economically, working in banks or law offices or hospitals, but their job satisfaction is nearly nil. These people are generally older than the typical college kid entering the industry. They have seen enough of life to finally recognize that they need to take a new direction while they still can. They are looking for a better fit—because one size does not fit all.

It just so happened that I found my niche in the information technology field. It was an industry I knew nothing about—but I knew it was on the upswell. It took me awhile to learn the business, but eventually I was able to ride the wave to success. My satisfaction came from doing my best to ride that wave. Another day, another time, and I might have played a different game. My true passion was never IT, any more than it was the chemistry that I had studied in so much depth for so many of my youthful years. In my experience, you develop a greater passion for something the more you get good at it.

My true passion, as I have come to recognize, is to help others rise to a higher level than they might ever have imagined possible, whatever their endeavor. When that happens, the passion almost always follows for them.

You don't have to go it alone. Few people can rise very high without reaching for a hand to lift them and holding on tight. Don't think of such help as merely "scaffolding," as some call it, or temporary support that should be taken down once you are able to get from point A to B. I don't see it that way. I see the scaffolding as an enduring part of the structure. Instead of tearing down the scaffolding, we should all leave it in place to support others as they build their own better way. This can come by sharing your experiences with others or by volunteering to help them out. Sharing your scaffolding can be as simple as referring someone to a book or an organization that helped you. Remember, no one goes it alone.

My mom understands this. Through the years, she has overcome many difficult circumstances—and to this day, she reaches out to help others as she herself was helped. She left the scaffolding in place. I continue to see my family psychologist, whom I met in 1991 when I was seeking help for me and my kids. I do it for continued emotional support and guidance. I do it because I am thankful for having her in my life. And I do it because, in gratitude, I can contribute financially to her charity, Reclaim13, which helps survivors of sexual abuse and exploitation.

In this world of many needs, with so much brokenness, people often need more than something to prop them up. Not only do you not need to go it alone, but you can look out for others so that they don't need to go it alone either. My brother Steve—the same brother who called for harsh punishment for flash mobs—has an interesting take on the old saying that if you give a man a fish, you feed him for a day, but if you teach him to fish, you feed him for a lifetime. "Sometimes, you can't teach a man to fish," he once told me, "so that's when you fish for him. We've got to help those who can't help themselves." That's the Steve I know.

We all deserve the chance to reach for dreams. Searching for what fits you is a noble and necessary requirement for a happy and fulfilling life. Be prepared that others might present you with obstacles rather than with help. Some will try to get in your way, squelching your dreams with their own expectations. And, yes, sometimes life itself gets in the way, throwing down challenges for you to overcome. My hope for you is that you will not get in your own way. Keep trying on different sizes. Don't tell yourself that you will never measure up, or that it's too late for you, or that success is for other people. Play the hand you're dealt, and play it as best you can, and you can find success, and define success, in your own way.

THOUGHTS:

DEFEAT IS WHEN YOU GIVE UP

For four days, nobody had seen him. The only reason I knew that our son was still alive was because I had the password to login to his bank's debit card account. I could see what he was buying and when—and most of the transactions were at a Target store and a Walmart not far from the halfway house where he had been staying. I was able to roughly triangulate his movements.

My wife, Breeda, and a business partner, Jimmy, joined me as we went to the area to stake out the positions where we were most likely to see his car as he traveled from point to point.

Jimmy was the first to spot him. He was walking out of a gas station, carrying a bottle of Gatorade and heading to his car, which was parked in front of a house. After hurrying to the scene, I slid into the back seat with him, where I found him already half-conscious. He was holding a can of keyboard cleaner to his nose, and he struggled with me as I tried to take it from him. Scattered around him were dozens of the same cans, empty.

At age thirty-five, our son was deeply troubled. He was addicted to inhalants, had been fired from his job, and had broken up with the woman he had planned to marry. He rarely saw his friends or family anymore.

We later learned that his car had broken down and he had been living in it for four days, huffing for a high. I wondered if his brain would ever be right again. We took him straight to the hospital.

I had no idea what to do, but I did know this: I would not give up on him, and I would not give up on myself. His plight was also my plight, and my family's. I knew that Breeda would be there with me. I didn't have any answers, but I had support. I knew that, come what may, I would not stop trying. I would do my best to get him and all of us through this traumatic time.

I've been around long enough to know that life often doesn't give you answers. I didn't have answers when my business was faltering. I didn't have a solution to control the economic crises we faced. I didn't know what to do when my first wife wanted a divorce. I haven't even figured out how to play a better game of golf. So I certainly didn't have the answers to our son's troubles—but I knew that we would not give up.

In my library is a book called *Tough Times Never Last, but Tough People Do!* by Robert H. Schuller. It is about navigating hard times. Somebody gave it to me when I was going through my divorce, and it helped me to keep on keeping on. After reading it, I ordered several copies to give to people who were also going through difficulties.

This is my take on the advice from that book: Life is a process, and nobody has all the answers. If you think you have got it all right, you are wrong. Your best approach is to be in the moment. Your job is just to keep going. Life is a tough journey with no known outcome.

About one hundred thousand people—fathers and mothers, sons and daughters—die each year in the United States from drug overdose, according to the National Center for Drug Abuse Statistics. The pharma companies, distributors, and doctors who hand drugs out like candy are all complicit. But for me, this was no time to worry about blame. When facing past challenges, I always knew I would persevere and get through them—it was almost like a game. This time wasn't a game. It was my son's life.

On that day, when we found him stoned on solvents, I had no idea which direction to take, or what to try next, or what to stop or start doing. I was sad, scared, and clueless.

It was a long trek with him. There were five inpatient treatment programs, two outpatient treatment programs, five hospital stays, and at least two police interventions (one of which I called myself, only to be told there was nothing they could do). His sister lived near his apartment and had the unenviable task of checking in on him.

We made many trips to visit him during those programs. He went to dozens of counseling sessions, and Breeda and I often joined him. We learned a lot in those sessions. We listened to the stories told by addicts. We listened to neurologists describe what addiction does to the brain.

The saddest moments came as the addicts' loved ones asked questions such as, *Should I pay his rent or let him live on the streets? Should I cut her out of my life or keep seeing and supporting her?* The experienced therapist would often respond that there are no simple answers. Imagine how the parents, significant others, and friends felt upon hearing that no one could tell them what to do. Imagine the sadness, frustration, and helplessness we felt. It's true, though. Nobody has all the answers.

At his last halfway house, I would see him only once a week. I would take him to the nearby grocery store and give him $40 to shop for food for the week. That is about $6 per day. He got by on a lot of chicken and pork. He told me once that he was down to three potatoes, which would be that day's breakfast, lunch, and dinner. Weirdly, he seemed OK with that.

He seemed particularly happy one day when I called him. He was out for a walk in downtown Chicago. "It's beautiful today," he said. "You don't get days much better than this."

A couple weeks later, I found out what was new in his world. "I want you to meet someone, Dad," he told me. "I hit the jackpot!" He explained that he had a new sponsor to help see him through the twelve-step addiction recovery program, and this gentleman had been particularly generous with his time. A recovered addict himself, he had spent hours with my son on many days to help him get a better grip on what he was facing.

He made it through the program. He was in the halfway house for six months and was tested for drugs every time he returned to the building. After a while, he was chosen to run the Tuesday night counseling sessions for recovering addicts and their families. One night, a surprise guest dropped in. He didn't recognize him at first. It was a gentleman who had himself been through recovery. For years, he had stayed with the program to help others. It was Ringo Starr.

During my visits, I met some of the people in his group. They told me how helpful my son had been when they had started going downhill. He had worked with a few of them to get them back into an inpatient program. He knew that process well.

The decision to get healthy was our son's, and his alone. Months later, I asked him why he made that decision. "I had nothing," he told me. "I couldn't see friends and family. I had no place to live but that halfway house, and barely enough food to get through each week. I made some friends in the counseling sessions, but many of them didn't make it, Dad. They were there and then gone. The addiction took over their lives again."

All this time, I had been thinking I wasn't giving up on him. And I didn't. But what mattered more was that he wasn't giving up on himself. In his heart, he always wanted to get better. He kept going back to rehab, over and over, willingly. He had the support of his family, but it was he who decided to make the change. It is him who gets the credit for sticking with it.

He got a job as a junior associate with a mid-size company. He committed himself to working hard for his new employer and has been rewarded with several promotions. He is loyal and thankful for the opportunity they gave him, and his career continues to flourish. Along the way, he adopted a dog from a shelter and seems well adjusted and happy.

Our son's journey taught me an important lesson: There are no reliable answers about what tomorrow may bring, although plenty of people still are quick to offer advice on what to do or not do. I would go so far as to conclude there are no right answers to much of what we humans face day by day, and the best we can do is attempt to advance by trial and error. We are not defeated unless we give up even on that.

I agree with the counselors when they say, "It's complicated." In their wisdom, they understand the importance of taking life one day at a time. And so we go, step by step. It's a parade of the present. There is always something to be done today.

As I think back on the life challenges that I have known, my son's addiction was the hardest I ever had to face. I remember it all, as vividly as if it happened yesterday, and those memories will not go away. I don't want them to. They give me empathy for families going through the anguish of addiction—and the fear, so often a reality, of losing a loved one.

The past, good and bad, is part of me. I want to remember, always, what it felt like to be helpless. It humbles me. It keeps me from becoming one of those people who think they have all the answers. No one does. We can only figure it out day by day, finding our own way, leaning on one another for support. Come what may, our job is to keep on going.

THOUGHTS:

SUCCESS OR FAILURE? ALL IN HOW YOU LOOK AT IT

Years ago, I was talking with a fellow at a party and asked about his kids. His face beamed with pride. His son had been captain of his high school football team and got a full scholarship to a Big Ten school where he graduated magna cum laude. Now he was making big bucks at a New York financial company. His daughter was equally impressive.

Realizing he was going on about their accomplishments, he paused. "How about *your* kids?" he asked.

"Mine? They're average," I said. "My kids are the kind that make yours look good." After a moment of awkward silence, I rescued him with a smile and told him that mine were doing well, too.

Nothing is wrong with being an average kid, though. In fact, it's a matter of simple math and logic: If there weren't a lot of average ones, we couldn't have any above-average ones. For every quarterback of a football team, there are fifty-two guys who are not. Most young people don't get national merit scholarships. Not everyone can, or should, excel by studying the theoretical physics of electron distribution (been there …).

Our society has a narrow definition of success. We burden our children with the expectation that they will all make it to the top—which, of course, is impossible. Our infinitely stupid solution, in recent years, has been to give a medal to every kid on the fourth-grade soccer team, no matter how they perform. We hand out "A" grades like Halloween candy. Instead, we should tell our daughters and sons that it is OK not to be the best at whatever they are doing. We should assure them they can try many other things that they really might be good at and enjoy.

Who are we as parents, or as a society, to decide what our kids' success should look like? If you are familiar with the *Ted Lasso* television series, consider the character Jamie Tartt, whose dad is never satisfied with his level of play. We have all seen moms and dads standing on the sidelines at baseball and soccer games, screaming at their kids that they're not doing it right. How sad is that? And yet aren't we all, to some extent, guilty of that competitive quest for perfection?

Instead of judging our children, we should be helping them find their own road to success and happiness. Sure, maybe your child will wear a lab coat and win a Nobel prize—and if that is their talent and passion, fine. Or maybe you have raised a mechanic with a knack for diagnosing what ails an engine. Or a dental technician who enjoys helping people to keep on smiling. If your kids love what they do, and if they give it their best, then you should feel good about their happiness and success.

I made the mistake of telling my daughter Jennifer what I had said to the man at the party who was extolling his children's accomplishments. It was a few years after the fact, but she didn't think it was funny. To this day, she often answers my phone calls with: "Hi, Dad, this is your *average* daughter." I'm proud of her. But her comment, though lighthearted, reflects our culture's narrow definition of success. I, too, have fallen into that trap. Is this fixation on being the best what we really want for our kids?

From a young age, we learn to judge ourselves by successes and failures—"the thrill of victory and the agony of defeat," as Jim McKay succinctly put it in his opening words on *ABC's Wide World of Sports*. The winners get their medals and glory, while those who failed to win, even if they came close, stand aside in frustration.

How long does success last by that measure? A brief, shining moment—about the time it takes to get the medal and hear the congratulations. Failure, too, lasts only minutes, and then it's back to families and friends and day jobs. Real life begins again.

Those fleeting moments that we so often call success and failure are false idols. They are just snapshots in time. Much more meaningful is what you are doing before and after those moments. What did you do to get there? And once that moment has passed, the question then becomes, What do you do next?

Golf is one of my favorite competitions. I've had the good fortune of playing with guys I have known for as long as fifty years and more. The win or the loss is often determined on the last hole. Someone makes a putt; someone misses a putt. The losers congratulate the winners and give them twenty bucks, and the winners buy the losers a beer. Then we tell stories about the round we just played, the good shots and the bad. The true enjoyment comes during the four hours we competed, each team fighting to get ahead, not the five minutes of fame at the end of the game.

On occasion, the competition is a blowout. One team is down so much that it is virtually impossible to come back. The game is over. I would much rather lose a hard-fought golf match than be up by two hundred points halfway through and win in a blowout. I love the competition far more than the victory.

For all of us, life is about the trip along the way.

We have all experienced disappointments in life. The promotion you didn't get. The relationship that didn't work out. The friend who let you down. But disappointments go away. You did your best. Now you can get on with your life, and you have no idea what is in front of you. Pretty exciting.

I think again of my own ups and downs—starting my company in 1989, broke and divorced a few years later. Pretty good start, huh? And even though both my business life and my personal life then took a turn for the better, I was broke again in the dot-com crash, and again in 2010 in the aftermath of the recession.

Right about now, you are probably thinking I was a pretty crappy leader. Hard to disagree with that assessment. I just knew that I had to keep on going. I had to find a way to make it work. It never dawned on me to quit trying, and I never thought of myself as a failure. Never was I mad, sad, or feeling hopeless. Those decades were a great time in my life. I had my kids, I had close friends, and I got up every morning with a mission.

On his Sunday morning TV show on NBC, host Willie Geist includes a regular feature called "A Life Well Lived." It focuses on people who have recently passed away—but the story isn't so much about what they accomplished as about how they conducted their lives.

Geist always finishes these stories with the observation that this was "a life well-lived." Instead of thinking about those moments where you felt like a success or a failure, look at yourself through the lens of how you lived your life.

We should never think of ourselves as a success or failure. We should look at life as a continuum. There will always be high points and low points along the way, but most of the game is between those points. Almost everything happens between the thrills and the agonies. What counts most is the way you play the game of life.

THOUGHTS:

SECTION TWO

FINDING YOUR OWN WAY

Even amid uncertainty, we have choices. We can decide how to respond to the unexpected and find our own path. Stuff happens. We can't undo the past, and the future is unknowable—but right here, in the present, we can decide what we will do to get to the next point. No matter what has happened, we can move forward with integrity. We can find strength within the chaos. The essays in this section are about finding resilience.

"What We Make of It" is a reflection on how I built my life—and an invitation for you to consider your own story. In reviewing who we were, we can find clues to what has shaped us into who we are, and that perspective helps us decide who we want to be. As I recap my own journey, think about your own life and what you can make of it.

In **"The Resilient Spirit,"** I share stories about rebuilding. For me, the rebuilding came after a series of financial setbacks, a divorce, and becoming a dad again unexpectedly. I know that many other people endure far greater challenges, but the lesson is the same: You can't control the past or the future, but the present is yours to shape.

"Choosing Your Inputs" is about how you can shape your todays. Who and what do you let into your life? What will strengthen you rather than weaken you? Your experiences wire your brain to think and respond in a certain way, whether positively or negatively—and you can rewire it by making the choices that are best for you.

"Strength in Routines" explains how you can put part of your day on autopilot. By cultivating routines, you can accomplish a lot of minor tasks and get them out of the way without giving them much thought. That way, you can devote more time to what matters most.

"Own Up, and the Rest Is Easy" explores the power of personal accountability. It's easy to blame others when something goes wrong—but why waste a perfectly good mistake?

"The Day I Grew Up" tells the story of the moment when I finally realized that I needed to stop screwing around and take control of my life. You may recall a turning point like that. For me, that day came in Vietnam.

"Put In More than You Take Out" is the number one rule for living a good life. When you help others and expect nothing in return, you tend to get something anyway—not necessarily in kind, but often in kindnesses.

"Passion or Talent: Which Comes First?" "Always follow your passion!" people often say. Sounds nice—but it's not that simple. Sometimes, passion comes along after you discover you are really good at something—and can make a living at it.

"When One Stands, We All Rise"—and when we stay silent in the face of injustice, we all suffer. This essay is a plea to stand up for what's right. What happens to any one of us happens to all.

THOUGHTS:

WHAT WE MAKE OF IT

Like everyone else, I've had my ups and downs on this roller coaster called life. By this point it should be clear that I believe much of what happens to us is a crapshoot, but that doesn't mean we are utterly lacking in control over anything.

I will pause now to take stock of the days that I have known. Bear with me as I run through a brief history of my zigs and zags, some of which I've already related and some that I will revisit later. I'm trying to pull it all together here as I look for perspectives on what it was all about. I hope you will do likewise and take a close look at your own story as I tell you mine.

I was fifteen, the oldest of five children, when my mom passed away. My dad did his best with my brothers and sisters. As for me, I was on my own. I had no direction. So long as I didn't get into trouble, I could do whatever I wanted. I made some good choices in high school, joining the golf team and becoming president of my fraternity. I held a job. I had a car and lots of dates. Life was good, right?

I wasn't mature enough for college but somehow ended up there by default, almost flunking out after a year. Next stop was Vietnam—not the path most young people wanted to take. My job in those jungles was to calculate the trajectory for howitzers, which was a whole lot better than being the guy loading them. It occurred to me that I should get serious about life.

Back in the States, I returned to college life at Southern Illinois University, nearly broke but grateful that the Army no longer owned me. Some friends let me live in their basement, where I ate their leftovers. More than once I lied about losing money in the cigarette machine in the student union, and the 55-cent refund got me a cup of soup and a Coke. Later, I got a $200 emergency loan from the school for food. When that ran out, I resorted to shoplifting at the grocery store. (I found it easy to tuck a can of tuna under my belt, but a package of ground beef? Not so much.)

Most days I hitchhiked the six miles to the university. Soon my girlfriend came to town to get her master's degree, and we shared half a trailer. She was broke, too—but we hit the jackpot when a friend got a job as a cashier at the grocery store. She scanned only about every other item. One day we saw that the store had mismarked all the steaks at 19 cents a pound instead of $1.19, so we loaded our cart. My girlfriend demanded that the manager honor the lower price, and we invited all our friends for a feast.

When I was out of new survival ideas, I hitchhiked home and asked my dad for a loan. It was one of the most embarrassing moments of my life, but he didn't hesitate. He gave me $1,000, asking no questions. "Keep it," he said, and I saw in his eyes something that looked like pride. I think he understood how I had made my own way since age fifteen.

Seven months after I started school, I got my first check, about $1,400, from the government, which was paying my tuition plus $200 a month. My girlfriend was working at Penney's by then, and later I got some extra pay as a chemistry research assistant. No longer on the brink of survival, we cleaned up our act. We even rented a house for $135 a month.

I finished college in 1976 and got a summer position with 100 percent commission at a job placement company. I ended up staying there, and why not? I was making more money than I had ever dreamed—$30,000 in my first year, twice that in my second. I had married by then, and we bought a house—and along came a baby in 1977.

Life was good until 1980, when the oil embargo hit. Most of my clients were plastics companies that found themselves without access to the oil they needed. My wife was not happy, but we got a second mortgage and survived. In 1989, I started my own technology company, plowing all our savings into it. We struggled again. My wife left me. From her upbringing, she was very security conscious, and I hadn't been respectful of that. I sold our house, downsized, and pared expenses at the company to bare bones.

The divorce forced me to use my 401(k) retirement fund to survive. I even kited a couple of checks to cover bills. The IRS froze my bank account because cashing in the 401(k) early left me with a tax penalty, which I was able to negotiate down from $32,000 to $10,000.

My company survived, and business was better after the mid-1990s. In 1995, I bought a run-down house and refurbished it with my brothers' help. A few years later, along came Claire. I was forty-seven and single when I became a dad again, but Claire's mom and I cooperated to raise a beautiful baby. All in all, it was a great experience.

In 2000, though, with the dot-com crash, times weren't good for a technology company. I had to rent my house to another family while my children and I rented an apartment for a few years until the economy improved. Again, I got a second mortgage.

Then, after being single for fifteen years, I fell in love with one of the kindest people I have ever known, and we married a year later. Breeda and I soon had a beautiful, blended family of seven children: my three and her three, plus her son's college friend, Nicole, who had recently lost both her parents.

"Nicole's part of the package," Breeda told me as our relationship developed, and I soon understood why she felt that way. When I met Nicole, I observed an outgoing young woman who had become a bright light shining over the family, and she remains so to this day.

Several years ago, Breeda and I, along with her son Anthony, sat down with Nicole at an outdoor breakfast table in Chicago's Lincoln Park. "We want to adopt you," Breeda said. "You are our daughter." Nicole looked into her eyes, then mine. "You have always been part of this family," I said, "and always will be." Nicole cried.

After marrying, we bought a nice Victorian just down the street from the house I had refurbished. Times were good—until about 2010, during what became known as the Great Recession, when my company lost two-thirds of its business. Once again, my family moved out of our home and rented it out for two years while the economy recovered. My wife, being an old-fashioned Irish girl, stuck with me, never complaining once about the moves we made to survive. It was always "game on," with no room to complain or feel like a victim. I was awake at seven o'clock in the morning and at work by eight every day, striving to be a good example of resilience.

As I thought about the ups and downs, I noticed that I had been in survival mode during any year ending with zero—1980, 1990, 2000, 2010—so it was with trepidation that I anticipated 2020. In 2017, I had the good sense to turn over the leadership of my company to my vice president of sales, Richard Walker, a good friend. And then, right on target, the COVID-19 pandemic struck in 2020. The curse of the zeros. *Again.* I credit our newly minted CEO and his team for doing a remarkable job of navigating the pandemic. Our consultants could work from home, and we survived in a lot better shape than many other companies.

This may sound insane, but through it all, I never had a bad day. I had my kids, my family, my friends. I woke up every day knowing what I needed to do, even if I had no idea how. My job was to figure out how to get from point A to point B. My job was to be a good parent, a good friend, a good leader for my company.

A lot happened as I made my way, and not all of it was pleasant, but each day built toward the next. I've appreciated every day of my life, good times and bad. In fact, sometimes the bad things in life lead to the good things. What matters is not what happens to you but how you choose to conduct your life.

As for me, I have chosen to live in the present, trying to make each day a little better for me and those around me. Regrets are for the past. Dreams are for the future, but it's only in the present that you can pursue them. Today is your opportunity to savor each step. Life is what we make of it as we find our own way.

Think about how you tell your own story. You can't change what happened, but you can change the way you think about it. You can consider it all part of what made you who you are today. I never wanted to be in Vietnam, for example, but those experiences shaped me. I learned I would have to work hard and to apply myself. I grew up there. More on that later.

As I write this, it's 2024, and I am in my seventies. It has been one crazy ride, and I'm still buckled up to enjoy whatever comes next. We are doing well, at present—and the next zero year is far away.

THOUGHTS:

THE RESILIENT SPIRIT

You've been there, I'm sure. The phone rings, and a moment later, everything has changed. The call can come at any time. For Mary Jo Carr, it came on a summer morning in 2006 as she was getting ready for a family reunion.

The caller was her oldest son, Mike.

"Mom ..." He didn't have to say much more. She knew something was wrong.

"What happened?"

"Mom, it's about Jeremy, he's—gone." She struggled to grasp the details. There had been an accident. Her grandson was driving on a winding country road, on his way to see his girlfriend. Something distracted him. His car hit a tree.

At the age of twenty-seven, her grandson was dead. At the funeral, my mom sat next to her son Pat, the young man's father, trying to console him and his wife as best she could on the loss of their child. She set aside her own grief and thought of others first.

That's Mary Jo Carr through and through—and I know her well. I have known her, in fact, for over half a century, since I was a teenager. She is my stepmom. I call her Mom.

My mom knows what overcoming is all about. She tells me that all things happen for a reason, that God has a plan. I don't know about that, but I do know she has experienced her share of grief and troubles. Her first husband left her in 1959 with five kids to raise on her own, one of them just six months old. Her son Kevin suffered severe brain injuries on Labor Day 1976 when he crashed his motorcycle, partially paralyzing him. Two years after her grandson's death, her son Pat died when a blood clot hit his heart shortly after hip surgery. A year later, Mike, the oldest son, died of brain cancer. Another death, another ring of the telephone. After thirty-four years of marriage to my father, she lost him to a lung disease in 2002. Almost twenty years later, her life partner, Dick, died of cancer in 2022.

Mom is ninety-four as I write this and is adjusting to life in her own apartment in a senior community. In all the decades that she has been part of my life, I have never (yes, never) heard her complain. Every morning, she reads a short passage from a little book titled *Jesus Calling*. Those are the thoughts that she chooses to put into her mind at the start of each day. She has the energy and mental acuity of someone half her age. She has an aura about her that invites others, even new acquaintances, to share their problems. She listens, asks questions, and often offers her perspective. That has long been her way. I call her "the mayor."

My mom has what I call "true resilience." She understands better than anyone I know that life is not a straight line—and so she is mindful to live in the present, choosing her daily inputs to maintain that perspective. She knows that is the key to a better life.

People who are resilient do not dwell on what happened to them or what they think happened to them. They do something about it. When you develop resilience, you come to believe that you can make a difference in your life. Resilience is hope.

When you run into a roadblock, you have two choices. You can stop dead in your tracks, or you can find a way around it. A lot of people just turn back when they hit a roadblock. Some feel unworthy, whether in the eyes of others or in themselves. Some feel like failures, forced into the one-size-fits-all mold and unable to break away to be themselves. Others lost the zip code lottery and feel their fate is stamped on them forever.

The resilient spirit brings a new perspective. You become curious about where the road ahead will lead you. You feel free to choose your own path. Even if your mother is on crack and your brother is a dealer, they don't define who you are. Even if society insists you should marry, buy a house, and have two kids, you can try something else on for size.

How do you develop resilience? It's easy for people to reassure you that, yes, you are worthy, you deserve more, you can bounce back—but how do you do it? When you feel stuck, you need more than words to get some traction. You need action.

Like so much else in life, progress comes one step at a time. You have control over the daily inputs that can rewire your brain to believe in possibilities. For starters, don't listen to any of the negative people suggesting that life is stacked against you; that you don't stand a chance. That includes the voices in your own head whispering that your situation is hopeless—because hope is what will get you through.

Resilience starts with being in the present. It's a lot like the movie *Groundhog Day*. Every day represents a new start. Actually, every minute is a new start. When you focus on the present, nothing else matters. Maybe you just lost your job—but for the moment, that doesn't matter because you and your little daughter are coloring pictures together. Maybe your spouse left you—but never mind for now because you are watching the sunset or talking with a friend.

Even when life seems out of control, you still own the moment. Every day you get to pick your inputs, one at a time. Yesterday and tomorrow don't exist when you are in the present—which, as I like to say, is where we live our reality. It is the only place you can be. You can't stay back in the past or skip ahead to the future. You can't change what happened to you, nor can you know what will happen next. Worrying about either will suck away your energy.

It's the here and now that is yours to define, and your choices will make all the difference. Think about how you start your day. What works for you? Some people pray or meditate, some people read, some people write down their plan for the day. Others get a cup of coffee and go for a walk. What matters most is that it's you who makes the choice. And if things go downhill, tomorrow will soon be a new today. You get to try again—seven new starts every week.

Once you rekindle hope and see real possibilities for yourself, you will feel motivated to persevere, even as life continues to throw challenges at you. You can bounce back—but not in a Rocky Balboa kind of way, struggling to your feet to face more punches. You can bounce back because you are living in a state of anticipation. You are building the future. That's what makes the present so exciting. It is under your control. The choices are all yours.

THOUGHTS:

CHOOSING YOUR INPUTS

Vietnam rewired my brain. If I had been true to my youthful convictions, I would have had the courage to go to Canada or to proclaim myself a conscientious objector—but at the time, I didn't even have the wherewithal to stay in school to continue my deferment.

The Army soon sized me up, put a slide rule in my hands, and sent me eight thousand miles from home to cause as much death and destruction as I could manage. My job was to tell combatants when they could fire artillery and how and where to aim. Afterward, we all wanted to know the KIAs. How many Viet Cong had we killed in action? We were eager to know our level of "success."

Don't get me wrong. I hated what I was doing—at first, that is. As the weeks and months passed, though, I came to accept the killing. I acclimated to the culture, you might say. Eventually, anyone observing me would have believed I was not just accepting but celebrating my role.

I knew it was happening. I was aware that the relentless negativity of that dismal setting was invading my brain, rewiring it in a destructive way, and I was appalled. Even if a bullet or a shower of shrapnel didn't find me, I was at risk from an enemy rising from within. My mind was vulnerable, and I resolved to protect it from further attack. Vietnam would not define me.

This is how we humans try to make sense of the world around us. All day, every day, you are processing inputs. Your experiences and observations are wiring your brain. Everything that the five senses perceive becomes etched upon your circuitry for later reference.

Many of those inputs are good. You learn, for example, to appreciate a stunning sunset and good music. You admire a painting. You cheer for the home team. Through trial and error, you discover what works and doesn't work in your relationships. You learn how to love. At the same time, though, you must deal with the negative inputs that life will inevitably send your way. If that haze of negativity overpowers the positives, you learn how to hate. You learn to distrust, to complain, to fear.

All your perceptions—the good and the bad, the beautiful and the ugly—collectively become your unique way of seeing the world. All those inputs turn you into—well, into *you*.

So why, since I wasn't a killer at heart, would I have willingly engaged in such destruction? It would be easy to say that I was answering my call to duty, that I was under orders, that I was just doing my job. Or I could say that it wasn't actually *me* who launched the rockets. Rationalizing comes easy for all of us.

I now see that once I was in that role, once I was under the cover of the jungle, another mental wiring took precedence. It was a circuitry that governed much of my being then and that would do so for years to come. I was determined to do the best I could with the task at hand. I wanted to be good at something—and if it was difficult, all the better. That was what motivated me to accept and even embrace my role as an arbiter of the artillery.

What experiences had wired me to desire to tackle a difficult job and to do it well? I was awakening to the need to do something meaningful with my life. After all, there I was in Vietnam, in the line of fire. I was an expendable commodity. My superiors did seem to value my brainpower, though, and my ability to calculate and triangulate. Still, I was just a kid, without much education, and it was high time to prove myself.

You can ask yourself endless questions trying to understand what makes you tick. What did you experience that wired you a certain way? And once you became that way, what new experiences again rewired you? I recognize in myself, for example, another fundamental quality: I'm highly competitive as an individual, but my nature is to be part of a team, working collectively. Where did that come from? I don't know, but I might find out as I continue combing through my past. As one rewiring leads to the next, it's all part of the evolution of who we are and who we are becoming.

The inputs that have contributed to shaping us can be troubling. In his renowned 1937 book *Think and Grow Rich*, Napoleon Hill points out that most of us, when we first encounter violence, abhor it. We find it shocking. When we see it again, we still don't like it, but it no longer surprises us. Then, after experiencing the violence for a third, fourth, fifth time, we start to feel we understand it. We come to accept it, normalize it, and even embrace it.

Consider the Patty Hearst case of the mid-1970s. The 19-year-old newspaper heiress was abducted by a small terrorist group called the Symbionese Liberation Army (SLA). An enduring image of the decade is that of her as a rifle-wielding young woman participating in the robbery of a bank. Hearst later explained that she had been blindfolded and gagged in a closet for two months and then indoctrinated with SLA political literature. Her kidnappers, in effect, rewired her brain to accept their radical ideology. The phenomenon in which captives identify closely with their captors and their cause has become known as "Stockholm syndrome," so named after another 1970s kidnapping case, this one in a Swedish bank.

The Hearst case was an extreme example of rewiring, certainly, but it illustrates what happens to a lesser but persistent degree in our everyday lives. We can easily become numbed, by sheer exposure, to the deep problems swirling around us. We begin to normalize things that are very wrong. We come to believe things that just aren't true. The negativity that surrounds us becomes our way of seeing the world. It also becomes our way of not seeing it.

Daniel Kahneman is widely known as the father of modern behavioral economics, for which he was awarded a Nobel Prize in 2002. Among his research findings was this discovery about human behavior: The first time you hear something you know isn't true, you will reject it. The second time you hear the exact same thing, you believe it could be true—and if you hear it a third time, you will likely believe it is true, despite your initial impression. In other words, we risk becoming blinded to the truth, as Napoleon Hill no doubt would have agreed.

What that tells me—and what it should tell all of us—is that the human brain is defenseless against negative inputs. We are vulnerable to being swayed into believing what we know to be false. Advertisers understand this and count on it. Politicians know it too. So does anyone trying to convince you to doubt yourself or to overturn your convictions. Such attempts at rewiring can influence you for a lifetime. You can end up living a lie.

An old saying commonly heard in newsrooms is that "if it bleeds, it leads," suggesting that a story is likely to get better play if it involves violence or crime. Editors have long recognized that readers and listeners are wired to pay more attention to the bad stuff than to the good stuff. The gold standard in journalism is balanced, impartial reporting. Ethical journalism persists, but so does another unseemly sort that panders to its audience, building ratings by dishing out information known to be false.

Social media companies are some of the worst offenders. They make their money by getting people to spend as much time on their sites as possible. To that end, they play people like marionettes. They understand intimately how the brain works. They know the nature of addiction and how to cultivate it. Never mind the damage they can do. Never mind that cyberbullying has led to suicides, particularly among teenage girls. The money comes first.

That is why I do not participate in social media. My brain is not for sale. I recognize that social media is here to stay, so we need to at least keep up our guard. As you get bombarded with more than you ever wanted to know, ask yourself how it all makes you feel. Did somebody's post make you happy or sad? Hopeful or helpless? Peaceful or angry? You're dealing with an avalanche of inputs. Awareness is your best defense.

The good news is that you do have the power, in many cases, to pick and choose the inputs that you allow into your brain. You are not wholly at the mercy of the random flow of events. You have some say in the matter. Unlike Patty Hearst, who was force-fed her inputs, you can strive for a diet of healthy ones.

How do you accomplish that? How do you exercise some control over your inputs? The answer might seem obvious. What do you allow into your life? How well do you play the role of gatekeeper? With whom do you associate? What do you read, or view, or listen to? Ask yourself what kind of person you want to be, and then orchestrate your inputs to help you meet that goal.

You can only control the inputs, however. You cannot control outcomes. There are too many variables in that part of the equation to know how things will turn out. As Hill also noted, the only things you can truly control are the thoughts you generate. You have the final say about how you see things and what you think of them.

That said, inputs do have consequences, of course—not just for individuals but also, on a larger scale, for our whole society. And when things turn out for the worse, our society unfortunately seems much more concerned with trying to manage those outcomes rather than changing the inputs. We build more jails. We hire more police. Meanwhile, our educational system is in disarray, particularly in the zip codes where kids desperately need a better way.

Consequences are simply the outcomes of actions and events. They can be either good or bad, and might not be misfortunes at all. In fact, I believe that an unintended consequence is sometimes an unintended opportunity—and when one comes your way, you should recognize it.

When we look back on our lives, we see that we never planned so much of the good we experienced. Opportunities often come as unintended consequences. Think again about how you met your significant other. Maybe you planned it all out, like following a script. Or maybe, like many of us, it just happened.

I'm not saying you should be impulsive. But when an opportunity comes along, just stop and think: *Is there an advantage here?* Even if the immediate consequences could be challenging, slow down and take a long view of what might happen. What possibilities down the road might open up to you? How might your life change for the better?

I know how hard it can be to break away from our comfort zones. We become accustomed to our circumstances, even when they are holding us back. Life has a way of putting people in a box, and they tend to stay there. It's familiar to them. They may be struggling to survive, but what lies outside the box can seem scary. The only way you will get anywhere, though, is to climb out of that box. What's out there for you? I'm not suggesting you race off into the unknown—but look around. Get a better view.

You won't be able to run with an opportunity if you stumble at the gate. Don't shy away because you don't fully understand it or feel others are better suited for it than you are. I am still trying to make myself say yes to more things. I actually practice saying, "Sure, OK, let's do it." Challenges can bring out the best in you.

As I look back, I see many times when I have benefited from getting out of my own box. I seldom regret saying yes. My wife, Breeda, loves to travel, for example, and so do I—once she convinces me to go. Experiences matter more than things, she reminds me. Recently, a couple of friends and I saw an opportunity with a bar and grill in the Chicago area. I had no clue what I was doing at first (Breeda would agree), but I looked forward to figuring it out, and it's been quite an experience. It requires traveling there, too, from balmy Florida to a city that seems to get as cold as Siberia. (Not exactly my comfort zone!)

Finding opportunities in challenges is something my son-in-law Ryan understands well. Ryan had been successful at a large, well-known company, where the senior leadership valued him. Then came an opportunity to run an entire division at a smaller organization. He took the leap. For several years, he had solid success, until new leadership centralized some product lines. Ryan was out of a job, and at his level, opportunities were few. His manager at the first company wrote him several letters of recommendation, and Ryan carefully considered a couple of offers that didn't line up with his values. He knew himself, and "any port in a storm" wasn't how he handled adversity.

For six months, day after day, he persisted in his search. Then his first company contacted him. An opportunity had come up. They would be happy to have him back.

There are lessons there for all of us. What seems like misfortune might not be misfortune at all. Persistence pays off. Always do your best. Keep your eye on the prize. Remember who you are, and keep your inputs in line with your values. For Ryan, those are qualities that have helped him find his way—and that can help all of us through life's adversities.

Much of the time, it's a matter of perspective. You come to see that no matter how bad a circumstance seems, you will get through it—and that's because you've done it before, somewhere along your trip. I'm not saying put on rose-colored glasses. I am saying make sure you are seeing clearly.

By now, you probably know what I will say next: Buckle up and enjoy the ride. We have no other choice. Remember, life is not a straight line. So much of what happens is random—and the best you can do is exercise good judgment over what you will allow into your brain and your heart.

THOUGHTS:

STRENGTH IN ROUTINES

Every morning, I wake up to a day that begins with a series of small, seemingly insignificant tasks. My routine rarely varies: I get up, make my bed, take a long hot shower (which I have found to be a necessity at seventy-four), and then move on to my pills, lotions, and daily hairdo. Next, I put on my workout gear, even though I'm not always sure I'll exercise. While my coffee is brewing, I take care of my dodgy back with various stretches. Then I settle in with my coffee in the den, read my daily online newspapers, and dive into another chapter of the book I'm currently reading.

I can do these things without thinking. I don't have to plan them out. Ever arrive at work and don't remember how you got there? It's like that—and that's why routines are so powerful. They put the mind on autopilot. They free us from the clutter of constant decisions.

In his book *Think Like a Monk*, Jay Shetty says routines allow the mind to focus on what truly matters. We still attend to the small stuff, but it doesn't get in the way of the big questions in life—*Should I ask her to marry me? Should we have children? Should I change careers?* We gain the mental space to give these larger issues the attention they deserve.

Routines are all about efficiency, and efficiency buys us time. We all have the same amount of time each week to make our lives work, says Laura Vanderkam in her book *168 Hours: You Have More Time Than You Think.* So why do so many of us feel we never have enough time? It's because we consume so many hours with trivial pursuits. Sure, they've got to get done—but by automating them, we not only gain meaningful time, but we avoid the risk that we'll forget them or procrastinate. Some may think of routines as being locked into a rigid schedule. Instead, they allow us to make the most of our 168 hours each week.

Take, for example, a simple habit I adopted after getting married. My wife suggested that I should squeegee the shower doors every morning to avoid streaks. At first, I resisted. For the first fifty-seven years of my life, I never thought about doing such a thing. Not once. But after a few thousand nudges, I reluctantly started to squeegee, day by day. Over time, it became part of my morning routine, requiring no thought or effort. Now I admire how the shower doors look. It's a small task, seemingly unimportant, but one that gives me a daily sense of accomplishment.

This sense of accomplishment is not just psychological; it's physiological as well. Every small task completed releases endorphins, known as the feel-good hormones. They are neurotransmitters produced in the brain's hypothalamus and pituitary gland. They provide natural pain relief. When released, endorphins bind to opioid receptors in the brain. This reduces the perception of pain and can produce a feeling of euphoria, often referred to as a "runner's high."

Endorphins are chemically similar to opioids like morphine, though they do not carry the risk of addiction. In the case of addiction, the substance takes over. Maybe it's nicotine or caffeine. Or maybe it's opioids or the host of street drugs that plague our society. When the body experiences a high, it asks for more. You make the choice to say yes or no. If you're after a runner's high, yes might be a good answer. If it's a heroin high you crave, you need help.

A variety of activities release endorphins naturally: physical exercise, laughter, dancing, a massage, and even finishing small-but-satisfying tasks. Your brain rewards you with a dose of endorphins, so you want to do it again. When you finish an activity and get that endorphin hit, you feel motivated to keep that routine going.

Endorphins reduce stress and induce a sense of well-being. By interacting with the brain's limbic system, they help to regulate emotions. That's why you feel in a better mood and calmer during activities that release endorphins. Not surprisingly, science has confirmed that there is healing power in a hug, or a sunset stroll, or a romantic rendezvous.

As you can see, routines can add up to big benefits. They not only create a sense of order but contribute to contentment and well-being—and they're easy. Once you have a routine in place, it doesn't take much effort anymore. That frees you up to tackle bigger stuff—challenges that are more complex and creative, requiring more brainpower.

I consider James Clear's book *Atomic Habits* to be a bible for making good habits easier and bad ones harder. Two of the strategies he recommends are "habit bundling" and "habit stacking."

For example, to make my treadmill workouts more enjoyable, I watch golf videos at the same time. When I bundle the two activities together, the time passes faster—and being on the treadmill doesn't feel like a chore.

Or I might let myself have my morning coffee only after finishing my stretches. By stacking them that way, the coffee feels like a reward. It's something I want, coming right after something I'm hoping to make into a habit. Other examples: cleaning up the kitchen counter before eating the meal you just cooked. Or folding your laundry before sitting back to watch the ball game. Or even folding it *while* you watch the game—that would be bundling, and it would probably do wonders for your marriage, too.

Clear also emphasizes the value of partnering and social support to reinforce habits. Do you want to get in the habit of a daily walk? Set a specific time, and do it with a friend. That makes each of you accountable to the other—and to build habits, it makes sense to be with people who have similar goals. Or if you go for that stroll by yourself, use the time to also call a friend—that's bundling again. You might get so lost in the conversation that you will walk farther and not even notice.

Another of Clear's strategies to reinforce a habit is to make things obvious—that is, to increase your awareness of the habit you want to develop. Let's say you want to practice your guitar every day. Put it where you can see it as you go about your day, not in a closet. As the authors of the book *Nudge* also pointed out, if you want to eat more fruits and veggies, store them on your refrigerator shelf in plain sight, not buried in the crisper drawer.

The converse is also true. If you want to break a bad habit, get the temptation out of the way—put it someplace less obvious. If you want to avoid bingeing on ice cream, keep it buried at the bottom of the freezer. If your spouse gets annoyed when you fiddle with your phone during movie night, leave it in another room. I turn my phone off before going to bed and before a round of golf. Everybody, including me, is happier that way.

When you look at your own life, I am sure you can find many ways to put those principles to work. They are simple steps, really. What's harder is how to train yourself to start thinking that way. As Daniel Kahneman explains in *Thinking, Fast and Slow*, the brain has two systems. One is for fast, automatic thinking, and the other is for slow, deliberate thinking. Routines are part of the fast-thinking system. They allow the slow-thinking system to handle those tasks that call for reflection and problem-solving.

Routines, in short, help your life to flow efficiently. When you turn them into daily habits, you are buying time to engage in the kind of creative, big-picture thinking that makes life more meaningful, more productive, more interesting. Ironically, routines help you achieve far more than a routine existence.

THE VICTORY OF MAKING YOUR BED

When I was a soldier in Vietnam, making my bed each morning was a daily requirement—and one that gave me comfort. In the chaos of war, you appreciate structure. You find reassurance in routines that you can control.

In his book *Make Your Bed: Little Things That Can Change Your Life ... And Maybe the World,* William McRaven, a retired four-star admiral and former Navy SEAL, says that making your bed is a task that sets the tone for the rest of your day. If you do it well, you can proceed with a sense of pride and accomplishment. It inspires you to take on more tasks, and tougher ones, as you go about your day.

McRaven sees the discipline of making your bed as a meaningful step toward a productive and fulfilling life. You are setting a standard for approaching other tasks. Discipline, order, and attention to detail are qualities essential to success, he says. They matter in battle, and they matter in everyday life.

The admiral's message in *Make Your Bed* is that success arises from small and consistent actions. Attending to those tasks builds the resilience and discipline to overcome larger challenges. When you start your day with a small win, you set yourself up for greater achievements through the day.

THOUGHTS:

OWN UP, AND THE REST IS EASY

At age fourteen, I decided to join a fraternity at my high school—yes, a *high school* fraternity. Each week, the pledges had to complete a series of tasks for the members, cutting their lawns and running errands and such. If you didn't keep up, you would get a painful swat with a paddle for each task you failed to complete.

The pledges were quite familiar with the paddles that were used to punish them for their transgressions. Each of us was required to make his own. I asked my dad for help, and he rose to the occasion. He purchased a fine piece of cherrywood, and together we jigsawed and planed it to perfection.

"Why are we even doing this, Dad?" I asked at one point. "They're only going to break it over my ass. And cherrywood, really? It'll never break! Couldn't we make it out of something softer, like pine?"

He gave me a look. "William," he said, "if it's worth doing, it's worth doing right." He was being true to his perfectionist nature, though I found his enthusiasm somewhat alarming.

The final step for our project was three coats of urethane, which rendered the paddle into a glistening thing of beauty. I won the best paddle award, of which I felt weirdly proud. My father had apparently made an impression on me with his insistence on doing things right.

It wasn't long, however, before I was way behind on the tasks I was supposed to complete. I weighed my options. Bend over? Or bow out?

I approached my father. "Dad? You know, I've been thinking. This fraternity stuff might just get in the way of everything else I need to do."

He seemed less than impressed. "You didn't get your tasks done, did you?"

I looked at my feet. "No. And they're not going to be happy about that."

"You *deserve* to get your ass beat," he said, flatly. "You knew going in what could happen, so now it's time to face what you've got coming. And after that, go ahead and quit if you want to."

I decided to succumb to the swats—and with my honor restored, I somehow felt I didn't need to quit after all. I soon caught up on all my tasks and then some. A few years later, when I became president of the fraternity, one of my first acts was to do away with the butt-bruisings. It was hard to see what was gained from kids smacking one another.

My dad taught me a tough lesson, though. When you make a commitment, keep it. When you screw up, admit it—and accept the consequences, whatever they may be.

This lesson has served me well in business and in life. I have readily admitted my many mistakes and paid the price for them in a variety of ways, all while trying to keep a sense of humor. My aim is not to make the same mistake twice. I have been only moderately successful at that.

I refer to this exercise in honesty as "owning your own shit"—a bit graphic, I suppose, but it drives me nuts to see people making excuses about everything. They seem to need something or somebody to blame for all their misfortunes, big and small, and it's anybody but themselves.

Trouble is, once you turn away all blame from yourself, you can't solve the problem. If it's always somebody else's fault, there's nothing you can do about it. You miss out on the opportunity to learn something. You lose control over what happened because you failed to own it—and that can steal the joy of discovering a solution.

Whenever a coworker made an honest mistake, I never responded with criticism. Even so, some would often make excuses or blame others. At that point, I would tell them this: "Why waste a perfectly good mistake?" That's what I often told my kids, too, whenever it was clear somebody had made one. "Even if you know it's not your fault, don't spend so much time pointing fingers. If you can figure out a way to call it *your* mistake, then you can face it. You can work on solutions. You can turn things around instead of wasting time playing the blame game."

Instead of telling yourself, and everyone else who might listen, that you were helpless and a victim, you can instead choose a position of power. You will grow stronger as you review the various options that you might have considered—and the next time, you are very likely to get better results. Most likely, nobody will buy your sad excuses anyway, so why not maintain control over the outcomes? No matter who's to blame, what matters most is to look for solutions.

Whatever you wish to call it, the skill of self-reflection is among the most valuable tools I have ever learned. If you're looking for a more delicate way to say the same thing, you have plenty of choices: *Own up to it. Take personal responsibility. Be accountable. Step up to the plate.*

So many people get stuck in the circumstances into which they were born. Those circumstances can feel desperate to the point of despair. They may believe they are screwed forever, simply because they were born into the wrong zip code. Such an attitude is understandable when you look at the roadblocks people face through no fault of their own. They see how other people live: in neighborhoods where crime and drugs and violence don't seem to be a way of life, where residents have access to decent healthcare and good schools, where they can buy groceries somewhere besides a 7-Eleven. They see a better way—*But why even try*, they might wonder, *if I'm beat before I begin?* They come to accept the boundaries around them.

That's true even when the boundaries are more tangible than a zip code—such as the walls and bars of a jail cell. It's hard to hold on to hope when you are living with a label that society has slapped on you, be it "inmate" or otherwise. You can feel as if the system will always be against you.

When I say "system," I don't necessarily mean some deep state keeping you in bondage. Whatever you believe holds you back and keeps you down is the system. It's whatever you feel has unfairly labeled you as somehow unfit. There is certainly plenty of blame to go around, including the biases built into our society—racism, sexism, ageism, and homophobia, to name just a few. All those things put labels on people.

And sometimes, people put labels on themselves.

You have a choice. You can spend your energies railing against your unfortunate circumstances, whatever they are—for whatever good that will do. You can believe your situation is hopeless, and you don't stand a chance. Or you can hold on to hope, telling yourself you will find a way to take a step forward, to make some progress. Yes, there are a lot of things you can't control, but you can always control how you look at them. Nobody can force you how to think. You have the freedom to tell yourself: *This sucks, but starting right now, I will do something about it.*

Don't get me wrong. The system does have a long, long way to go. The nation's prison population, for example, is woefully lacking in education, which limits inmates' choices after they are released. Decades of research has made it clear that prison education programs reduce recidivism dramatically, with every dollar spent on education saving $4 to $5 on imprisonment costs, the *New York Times* has reported.

Unfortunately, that's a truth that can be hard for the public—and, therefore, politicians—to swallow, and the money instead flows to building more prisons. The government patches the problem rather than addressing its roots. Take healthcare as another example. We build more hospitals, and we pay out disability benefits, but how much do we invest in programs for early intervention and awareness? How much less might we be spending on disability benefits if people had better healthcare all along?

Whether hospitals or prisons, the solution shouldn't be building more but needing fewer. We have the capacity to plant the seeds of hope that can make change happen. It would be far better to reduce the recidivism that swells the prison population. I admire and contribute to a charity called The First 72+, which reaches out to newly released inmates with housing and other support. What these people do in the first three days of freedom, the organization points out, often determines whether they will return to jail.

Breeda and I are fortunate to be able to help other charities that plant hope. Earlier in this book, I mentioned Reclaim13, a nonprofit that my longtime family psychologist started. Reclaim13 rescues girls from the sex trade and gets them into a safe house where they can live full-time, with extensive counseling provided. We have donated for years, and I recently joined the board. Christopher House is another favorite charity of mine that I work with. It helps disadvantaged families by making sure they have a safe place to live and food on the table, along with support services such as day care for children as young as six weeks old. I have bought and delivered diapers and other supplies for several years and donate annually. Claire volunteered there for a summer while in college and took care of a caseload of families. She also volunteered at Jane Addams Resource Corporation for a summer, helping people write their résumés. This nonprofit trains people in high-demand manufacturing skills, such as welding, robotics, and HVAC maintenance, and places them in jobs. Many are recently out of prison, have had addiction problems, or just need a new start in life.

There are so many worthy charities like these, all working to make change happen. They help to meet our collective responsibility to assist those who are less fortunate. When choosing which ones to support, just follow your heart. It will lead you naturally to the people and places that are making a difference in the ways that are important to you.

Whether on a societal or an individual level, we must own up to what has gone wrong and start setting things right. We live in an age sorely lacking in personal insight. In *Think Like a Monk*, author Jay Shetty (who once was a monk) exhorts us to get in touch with our values by first setting aside life's external distractions, which often control our thoughts. By turning down that noise, you can take a look inside. Who are you? What are your values? What is important to you? What is your purpose?

To answer those questions, you need to mentally separate yourself, for a time, from the things that are happening to you, or that have happened to you, or that you fear will happen to you. Only by breaking free of the labels that others have put on you, and that you put on yourself and on others, can you clearly see the role you have played in the events of your life. You gain the personal insight that leads to personal responsibility. You no longer dwell on what happened to you. Your focus now is on what you can do about it. Your new focus is who you are, not how you are.

As for me, I might easily have blamed the economy for the business challenges I faced—such as when the bank cut our line of credit in half. Could it be that I chose the wrong time to be paying dividends? Did I hire too many people? Did I spend too much money in certain categories? Should I have kept more equity in the company? I have learned that you need to be comfortable saying "This is my fault" before you can take effective action.

How about you? Have you owned your own shit? Because once you do, the rest is easy—though maybe not as easy as you'd like. At least, though, you can start moving forward.

THOUGHTS:

THE DAY I GREW UP

As you look back through the years, you may recall the day when you realized you had grown up. You were an adult, with adult responsibilities, whether you liked it or not. Maybe it was when you got married, or became a parent, or lost a parent, or experienced some other turning point.

I remember not only the day but the moment I grew up.

In the spring of 1968, when I was seventeen, many of my friends had been accepted into college. My parents never really pushed the idea of higher education, but I figured I should probably do what my friends were doing. That March, I submitted all of one application, to Bradley University. I'd never heard of it and didn't even know where it was. In May, I got a letter saying the college had accepted me. I don't know why. My high school grades and SAT scores were nothing to brag about.

I soon realized that Bradley was a school for the well-to-do, which I sure wasn't. Still, my freshman year was great. I joined a fraternity. I became well-acquainted with beer. I learned to win at Hollywood gin. After one game, a rich friend told me that for my payoff, I could pick out whatever I wanted from his closet. I scored a suede blazer with leather elbow patches. Another payoff got me an old VW Bug without brakes.

I finished my freshman year with a GPA of 3.75. My parents were impressed when I told them. I didn't tell them that Bradley was on an eight-point system, meaning a 4.0 was a C. My grades were C's and D's, and all were gifts. Concluding that I wasn't ready for college, I came home and got a job as an apprentice butcher.

And then came the first draft lottery, on December 1, 1969. My birthday was the eleventh pulled. On January 21, I was in the Army.

I filled out a series of questionnaires. One of them asked something to the effect of whether I would rather jump out of an airplane or read a book. In my infinite wisdom, I chose "read a book." Then came a battery of tests—and they put me in a training program for Fire Direction Control. I had no idea what it was, but I soon found myself in a group of college graduates in their twenties who had signed up for three years to become officers. I was nineteen. I had one year of college with lousy grades. My goal was to get out of the Army as soon as possible.

In the training program, we learned the behavior of artillery shells once they are fired. We learned that where they land depends on a lot more than the aim. They spin like a football as they fly. The temperature, humidity, and wind speed all play a role. The planet's rotation, too. In high school physics, I had been lucky to get a C. This was like a 400-level college course and many times harder than any class I'd ever taken. *Should I even try?* Then I learned that the Army had a "Plan B" for those who didn't pass … I would be the one loading hundred-pound shells into 155mm howitzers. I thought that was a bad Plan B.

If I were to have a chance at making it, I would need to outwork my classmates. I had never applied myself so hard to anything. I gave it my all, and I passed.

My reward for all that diligence? I got to put all that book learning into action in Vietnam.

My flight landed in Củ Chi on an evening in mid-July. I could see flashes of battle fire in the distance. *This isn't good*, I thought. Walking down the ramp from the plane, I caught a strong scent of urine. Not a great first impression.

I spent my first three months in a base camp with banks of radios and dry-erase boards that displayed maps of the local region. On the boards we would mark down, in different colors, the location of all personnel. That way we knew where we could, or could not, fire artillery. We needed to track the US Army ambush sites, the US Navy boats on the Saigon River, the Vietnamese army and navy locations, and all the villages. We also kept track of curfew times. Three of us took turns manning the post 24/7.

There was no room for mistakes, and that's where the job got tough. When an Army patrol got into a firefight, they would yell over the radio for artillery support and give the coordinates. My job was to determine yes or no. Within seconds, I had to find the coordinates on the whiteboards and see who was where. If the request came in for a no-fire area, I would need to get permission from local authorities—army, navy, heads of villages, etc. If I couldn't get that clearance, I had to tell the patrol, basically, "Sorry, can't help you."

Did I mention I was nineteen years old? A boy deciding whether and where to rain down fire. Who thought that was a good idea? In my half century of life since those days, I have never experienced anything close to such pressure. One night, I got simultaneous calls, one from an Army patrol and one from a US Navy riverboat. They each reported being in a firefight—and when I checked the coordinates, I realized it was the same firefight. I explained over the radio why I would not be providing the requested artillery support. Actually, I screamed it: "Stop! You're shooting at each other!"

After three months, my next gig was out in the field with an infantry battalion of about two hundred men who would set up ambush sites at night. Our job was to provide howitzer support from our bunker.

To determine the proper aim, we used slide rules and charts. We were on duty three at a time: one for the charts, one for the slide rules, and a second lieutenant to oversee our calculations and decisions. I had turned twenty by then—still the youngest and least educated.

A few months into that gig, we got a field computer. It came in a big box and was untested and not to be trusted, not yet. We were to use it as a backup to our slide rules. There were several of us in the bunker. Some had no interest in the thing. A few did, including me. I wanted to be chosen to test out the machine in live combat exercises. I didn't know anything about computers, but I knew figuring it out would be tough. I wanted that responsibility. I wanted it badly.

They selected someone else. The choice made sense. He was older, and smart. He had four years of college. He had earned his degree—and me? One lackluster year before quitting. I was happy for him. He was my friend and a good guy. He deserved that job. I was not happy for me. I was crushed.

That was the day I grew up. My life changed profoundly the moment I learned that somebody else would get something that I wanted badly for myself. It was a clear signal that I must do something serious with my life. I had to work hard for the things I wanted. I took a look at myself. Sure, I was doing a good job as a teenage artillery controller—but I wasn't in control of my life. Basically, I was a college dropout who, as a consequence, had been drafted and sent to this hellish corner of the planet. It happened because I had no plan for myself. That had to change. I was done with screwing around and just getting by.

My final day in the Army came several months later, on September 24, 1971, four months ahead of schedule because the war was starting to wind down. I had served twenty months, and it was farewell to Vietnam, a lovely land of lovely people that was not so lovely for a time.

The day after I flew home to Chicago, I packed my bags and hopped on a train to Southern Illinois University in Carbondale (SIU). Why there? At all the other schools, classes were already well underway. SIU was on a trimester system, so classes had only started the previous week. I had $200 of savings in my pocket. I had no idea whether I could be admitted. I didn't even know where I would sleep that night. No matter. I had a few friends down there. I'd figure it out.

Upon arrival, I went directly to meet with the dean of admissions. I was a veteran, I told him, and had just gotten out of the Army a day earlier. I didn't mention my wasted year at Bradley.

"Which curriculum would you like to take?" he asked me.

"What's the hardest thing you've got?" I asked.

"Chemistry."

"I'll take it," I said. He paused, and I could see in his eyes what he was thinking: *This is a little strange*. Then he nodded. He had opened a door for me. I had no idea what was on the other side, but I couldn't wait to see.

My heart wasn't set on studying chemistry. My dad had been a chemical sales engineer, but I wasn't trying to follow in his footsteps. My heart was set on doing something tough and proving to myself that I was somebody. Chemistry was not yet my passion, though it became so once I found out I was good at it. I'd rather have studied engineering, but the school didn't offer it. Even so, my interest in engineering was just because I knew it was a tough field.

I ended up getting my chemistry degree and then completed all my master's classwork and research and a good portion of my PhD classwork. My research was in organometallic chemistry (don't ask). I discovered, by way of a math error during an experiment, a procedure for making a new class of compounds. I did presentations on my new discovery and won an interschool research competition.

To finish my doctorate after the summer break, I was supposed to work for a professor at the University of Massachusetts Amherst. It didn't happen. I needed a summer job, and one afternoon, a golf buddy referred me to his cousin, who owned a job placement company. The owner kept calling me—actually, badgering me—until I agreed to be interviewed.

This was 1976. The job was for 100 percent commission, and the application had asked how much I expected to earn in a year. I wrote down the ridiculous sum of $12,000. I made over $30,000, mostly placing technicians and chemists. I wasn't going to leave good money like that. I topped $60,000 my second year and $90,000 my third. I worked there for the next thirteen years, and I ended up responsible for most of the company.

And that's how my career was born. It just happened. If I had not chosen to play golf that afternoon, or if I had shrugged off my friend's suggestion, my life might look entirely different today. Instead, I got an opportunity, and without a lot of thought, I said yes to it. In 1989, the owner decided to reengage with his company, and we encountered some style differences. It was then that I decided to start my own company, but not one that would compete with his. I looked around and saw a big opportunity in the IT business. It was a large and developing market with all the rules already in place. I decided to say yes.

Who knew? Not me. I didn't plan it that way. I had expected to become a professor and a research chemist. Remember, life is not a straight line. Looking back, you too can probably see the defining moments that changed your trajectory. When you open a door, whatever lies on the other side could change everything.

By the way, I finished my bachelor's degree with a GPA of 3.43—and this time, it was on a four-point scale.

THOUGHTS:

PUT IN MORE THAN YOU TAKE OUT

One winter day in the early 1980s, my then wife and I headed out for a weekend at my parents' cottage near the shore of Lake Michigan. It had snowed heavily, so my parents came out on snowmobiles to pick us up just off the main highway. After a ten-minute ride through the forested hills, we arrived at their small cottage, its bright lights welcoming us.

No sooner had we unloaded than my dad grabbed a couple of bottles of white wine and got back on his snowmobile, motioning for the rest of us to join him on another jaunt through the woods. "Let's go!" he said, and he led us to another cottage. As we approached, I could see steam rising from an outdoor hot tub—and soon we were sipping the wine and relaxing in the pulsing water under brilliant stars.

"Boy, you sure do have nice neighbors," I said, smiling at my dad. And it was true. Whenever we had family get-togethers at my parents' cottage, there always seemed to be other cottages available for our use if we needed more space, and even extra snowmobiles at our disposal.

Dad nodded. "I take care of the neighbors," he said, "and they take care of me."

He explained that, since he and my mom lived full-time in that shoreside community, he often prepared the cottages for their owners' weekend arrivals—turning on the heat and lights, shoveling steps, and warming up the hot tubs.

"People can work with you or against you," he said, "and it's your choice which it is." The number one rule for a good life, according to my dad, is to put in more than you take out. "Putting others first," he told me, "has served me well all my life."

That principle has long guided me, too, in my life and work. We decide how much effort to put into our relationships. We can't control how much we get back, if anything—people will sometimes work with you, sometimes against you—but what we give is always our choice to make. When we give our best in good faith, the good that we send into the world can make a difference in ways we might never see nor understand.

At my daughter Jennifer's first job after college, the average stay for a new worker was only six months. The company paid reasonably well but expected workweeks of sixty to seventy hours—so when you broke it down, it wasn't all that much more than minimum wage. I told her how a friend, George, had once explained the secret to success: "When everyone else quits," he observed, "that's when they put you in charge! You just need to stick it out until you know every nook and cranny of the company."

I suggested to Jennifer that she give it two years to show what she could do. "After that, I bet you'll be able to have any job you want there," I said. She did stay, and the strategy worked. She discovered, after her initial hesitation, that she was good at managing people and had better leadership skills than she thought. In fact, she developed a passion for helping and leading others. She kept at it for five years, getting more and more responsibility, promotions, and raises. Though she had many other job offers along the way, she stayed and built her career at that company.

Eventually, the company was bought out and merged with another. While everyone else was complaining, Jennifer called the new management team and asked, "How can I help make the transition better?" They soon put her in charge of a large team responsible for customer retention worldwide. While others had left to look for a good job, Jennifer had decided to make her job good. It shows what can happen when you keep on keeping on. As she demonstrated, you need to do more than occupy space. You should do more than is expected of you, even if it's more than you expect to receive. Always put in more than you take out. My dad surely would have agreed.

A sales trainer once told me a tale of two women who decided they didn't like their company's culture and decided to quit. As a farewell gesture, they got up early during their final two weeks and brought in doughnuts every day to share with their coworkers. There must have been something magical in that doughnut dough, because the two women soon found their popularity surging. At the end of those two weeks, they decided they didn't want to leave the company after all. The culture had abruptly turned friendlier.

I relate that tale not because I think you should go broke buying doughnuts to buy friendships, but because it makes a good point about the importance of relationships. When you give something of value to others, they tend to give something back—not necessarily in kind, but often in kindnesses.

That's solid advice that transcends careers. I have often told my children that their primary job is to make the world a little better by their being in it. That might be through charitable work or philanthropy, but such a contribution often comes simply by meeting the challenge of raising good kids with good attitudes who, in turn, will raise such kids themselves. It comes in the give-and-take of our relationships as we build the bonds that endure. We have done our jobs when we can say, at the end of the day, that we had more deposits than debits in life's moral bank account.

It's not about looking for the good life. It's about making life good.

When you develop a strong relationship with people and help them with their needs, they will want to do the same for you. When you offer your assistance out of kindness, people will sense that you are authentic. They will see that you aren't expecting anything in return—but it comes, nonetheless.

That's a powerful life strategy, and it is a great way to build a business, too. It works whether times are good or tough. At York Solutions, the IT company that I founded, professional development and community-building have long been a priority. The company doesn't benefit financially from those efforts, at least not directly—but the goodwill comes back to us manyfold.

At one point in 2010, in the aftermath of the deep recession, I got a call from our CFO on a Friday afternoon, just as I was heading out of town. "I need $350,000 by Monday to meet payroll," she said. I asked her to give me a couple of hours, then started dialing for dollars. I didn't yet know how I was going to do it. A few phone calls later, I was able to assure her that the money would be in the bank first thing Monday morning. I had no trouble getting a favor from people who knew me, liked me, and trusted me.

My successor as CEO, Richard Walker, is a master at putting the relationship development principle into action, and he wrote a book about it: *Relationship Equity: Your Cornerstone Investment to Great Gains in Business and Life*. "We do well by doing good," he often says. One of his book's central themes brings to mind my dad's advice: People can work with you or against you—and it's your choice which it is. The way to build relationships is to give generously of yourself. That sentiment is why Richard and I are longtime friends.

In my over forty years working as a manager, I have focused on hiring people of good character, which I saw as even more important than the skills they exhibited. Skills matter, of course, but they can be taught on the job. A generous spirit and commitment are another matter. If character can be taught at all, it happens long before people enter the workforce.

For decades, I extensively interviewed every person who joined our company. I wanted to know who they were. What had influenced their lives along the way? What was important to them and their future? I needed to find out how to help them achieve their goals. I didn't think of them as employees but rather as business partners from day one. They weren't just people who worked for York. I wanted York to go to work for them. I wanted to help them personally and professionally, and that requires more than a superficial relationship.

I kept an eye out for the kind of teammates who consistently did more than we asked or expected of them. I looked for those willing to invest time in helping others succeed. I tried to make sure to give them more responsibilities and more money before they had to come to me and ask—and before they left for greener pastures. I recognized that those employees were destined for leadership because they were eager to put in the work—to "earn their stripes," as they say.

I felt inclined to help people who themselves were helpful and who didn't think they deserved a promotion simply by hanging around long enough. Sometimes people expect help but seem unwilling to help themselves. They want the perks without the work. Their managers can wear themselves out trying to help them.

Here's the advice I shared with people who wanted to become managers: Don't hope for a promotion so that you can show what you can do down the road. Show what you can do now. Play the part right away, whenever you can. Your own supervisor no doubt feels overwhelmed at times, so lend a hand with some of the easier responsibilities. You will gain experience, and the bosses will likely appreciate and reward what you do. If they don't, some other company will.

The desire to help others is built into our DNA. That's why we live in communities. We need human interaction—people in tight-knit communities live longer, as multiple studies have shown. In one way or another, we are created to be caretakers. Some people give dollars to the homeless on the streets, some give McDonald's gift certificates. Some don't do these things, but they contribute in other ways. My brother Tom buys two-for-one sandwich deals and gives one sandwich away. Some people travel far to assist victims of disaster, or they volunteer to help build homes for Habitat for Humanity. Some donate to charity. We seldom know the real impact of our gifts of time and money.

As members of a community, most people will want to help strengthen it. If some seem interested mostly in themselves, they deserve the benefit of the doubt. If whoever you are helping seems ungrateful, be patient. Don't misread them. It can take time for them to trust that you've got their back.

I understand the temptation to give up. Sometimes, a relationship can feel as if you're heading down a one-way street. I've felt that way. I've reached the point of thinking there's nothing more I could do—such as for my brother Tom as he struggled with life. (You'll see how that worked out when you meet him later, in my essay on the power of forgiveness.)

As a couple, Breeda and I have certainly felt frustration while trying to assist others. We repeatedly helped a friend who seemed to be making no progress. We felt discouraged, wondering if our support was worth it, but didn't give up—and his life turned around. He found happiness. He came a long way. Another time, we saw potential in a nineteen-year-old doorman at the downtown apartment building where we were living. The young man wanted to be an accountant but couldn't return to school because he owed fees. We paid those fees for him. Did it make a difference? Did he finish his degree and achieve success? We don't know. What we do know is that helping him was the right thing to do.

Relationships are similar to a bank account with deposits and debits—and you should always put more in than you take out. They also are like an investment, which is likely to eventually give you a return if you stick with it. Investments come at a risk, though, as we are so often warned. Sometimes you need to adjust where you devote your resources, but do so with caution. Maybe you'll see great dividends. Or maybe nothing. You can't be sure. No guarantees. All you can do is use your best judgment.

In a world where so much can go wrong, our job is not to control the outcomes, because we cannot. Our job is simply to put in more than we take out. Our job is to work with people, not against them—regardless of what they do for us. We shouldn't expect a payoff—a quid pro quo or a mea culpa. The words "How can I thank you?" and "I'm sorry" may never come.

If there is any payoff, it's the knowledge that we tried. We did not give up. We did our best in good faith. And maybe somehow, someway, someday, it will make a difference.

THOUGHTS:

PASSION OR TALENT: WHICH COMES FIRST?

I suck at golf. That's the truth. Despite playing the game for over half a century, taking a couple hundred lessons, hitting hundreds of thousands of practice balls, and spending countless hours on the range, my average score still hovers in the mid-'90s.

Many of my friends are single-digit handicappers, yet they rarely practice. They just play golf. For me, it's more complicated. I can't quit, no matter how frustrated I get by the fourth hole or how many different swings I try before the back nine. Why? Because I love the game. I've loved it since I was a teenager. I am passionate about golf, even if I might not have all that much talent for it. I'm not expecting to be a star. I golf because I enjoy it, and that drives me to want to get better at it.

I often have wondered how talent interacts with passion. I believed for a long time that if you have enough passion, talent will grow and vice versa. It's not that simple, though, as I have observed through the years. They don't come as a package deal. Much of the time, a passion is best expressed as an avocation, not an occupation—a hobby, not a living.

My daughter Claire had plenty of talent for golf. She started lessons at fourteen, and by her junior year, she was captain of her high school team. She could outdrive all the other kids and hit the ball almost 240 yards. Our golf pro even called her "the human rubber band."

Claire didn't much care for the game, though. She didn't show the kind of passion I brought to it. She didn't like beating other kids in competitions. By the time she got to college, she had walked away from golf without looking back. Instead, she became increasingly involved in a different talent—for social work. While still in high school, she went to Haiti to help hurricane victims and realized she was a natural when it came to helping others. With similar experiences, her talent and her passion continued to grow.

Some might say we are each born with a gift, a special mix of passion and talent, and that our mission is to discover that gift and put it to good use. But that's not usually the way it goes. Scott Galloway, an entrepreneur and professor of marketing whose books include *The Algebra of Wealth: A Simple Formula for Financial Security,* points out that only 2 percent of actors and 1 percent of musicians, for example, can make a living at their craft.

Your priority should be financial security, Galloway says. You should first focus on developing marketable skills. Do you have a raw talent that also meets a demand in the job market? Then work on developing that. Passion may come along later, he says. When you get really good at something, a passion for it tends to develop.

That's how it was for my dad. Tennis and sailing were his passions, but he needed to support a family—so he relied on his talent. Dad was a chemical sales engineer for the metal coating industry. He became so good at it that after he retired, he stayed on as a consultant at his customers' request. Taking good care of them had become a passion. He died at seventy-five of a lung disease likely caused by so many years of direct exposure to various chemicals while he was personally doing all he could to help those customers.

I see that pattern in my own life, as well. I do a lot of home remodeling work, even though I couldn't design a doghouse when I was younger. But after I tried remodeling a time or two, I discovered I had a talent that I hadn't recognized. As I learned more and did more, I gained valuable skills—and they certainly were marketable ones. I got to the point where I could walk into a house and, within seconds, visualize how the rooms could be reconfigured. Eventually, I felt the passion growing. It was a by-product of the talent and skills. The passion didn't come first.

As I look back, I see that this was also the case in other things I pursued. Take my would-be chemistry career. I spent years studying chemistry, even completing much of my PhD coursework. I was good at it, and had the skills to advance, but it didn't initially ignite a fire in me. Then, one day, I made a slight error in a calculation and produced a compound never before known to mankind. I was astounded when my professor told me what I had accidentally accomplished—and the next morning, I couldn't wait to get to the lab to try out new ideas. A passion for chemistry was clearly taking hold. I was looking forward to finishing my doctorate at the University of Massachusetts Amherst—until my lucrative summer job opened a different career path. It just happened, sort of the way creating that compound just happened. I didn't plan it.

I eventually found myself in business, focusing on the IT field—and that, too, wasn't about passion or talent at first. I barely knew how to turn on a computer. I did it out of necessity, to support my family, as IT was a rapidly expanding market. I worked hard, making many mistakes along the way. I learned from those mistakes, and as my skills grew, I found that I was developing a passion for starting and managing a small business. As time went on, I began to help others with their new and recent start-ups.

So what have I concluded about the interplay between passion and talent from these observations about golf, home design, business, and chemistry? Pretty much this: Talent and skills will often grow into a passion, but if your passion isn't leading you to financial security, it should not become your profession.

Carol Dweck, a psychologist known for her work in motivation and personal development, argues that we are not born with fixed measures of passion and talent. It's not that we either have them or don't. With persistence, we can develop both. With a "growth mindset," we will improve. Through effort, we learn and grow, says Dweck, whose books include *Mindset: The New Psychology of Success.*

Dweck emphasizes that a growth mindset doesn't mean being blindly optimistic. It means you recognize that growth comes through perseverance. You can see challenges, and even failures, as opportunities to do better. Instead of comparing yourself to others, you can be grateful that their achievements inspire you. Focus on persistence rather than results. Learning, in itself, is its own reward.

Thinking back, that's the attitude I have brought to my golf game. I have friends with far more natural talent who inspire me to put in the hours to get better. Even when I have a bad round, I can define it as a step forward. That's the growth mindset. In my business life, too, I have kept on showing up and giving it my best, even when I wasn't sure what I was doing. As Dweck sees it, such persistence eventually pays off. By keeping at it, you learn to get through whatever you are facing.

It's popular to say, "Just follow your passion," but it depends on where it's leading you—and if that isn't toward a successful career, change direction, Galloway says. When competence takes the lead, passion often follows. I didn't start out with a passion for business or home design. In both, I either took advantage of an opportunity or acted out of necessity. And then, as my skills grew, so did my interest. It was discovering I was good at something that drove me to do more, and that fueled the passion.

I get energy from the effort—not necessarily from succeeding. I think back to my first job as a restaurant busboy, which is a job one doesn't typically approach with a passion. As I worked with my friend and fellow busboy, Tom, we decided to turn it into a competition. That changed everything. I wasn't passionate about slinging dishes, though. I was passionate about doing the best job I could.

I discovered that I thrived on the excitement of a challenge. Later, when I got into business, I often felt bored after getting a project up and running. I would turn it over to somebody else to manage, and I would look for something new to get excited about. Once, during a bad recession, a business partner asked me whether I thought I was at my best when things were going well. "Probably not," I said. For some reason, I am at my best when times are tough and the game is on.

The Japanese word *kaizen* means "change for the better." It describes a workplace culture of continuous improvement and started with the auto industry in Japan. The philosophy encourages employees to constantly look for ways to improve processes and reduce waste, no matter how well something seems to be working. Shouldn't we all be doing this? Shouldn't we all be looking to do things better, whether on the job or in our families—or as citizens of society?

When you are changing for the better, you are on your way to success, whatever your mix of talent and passion. When you put in the effort, you are bound to find yourself continually improving—and that's a reward in itself. You will see the results. You will truly be enjoying your work. You will feel the passion growing.

There's no formula that works for everyone. One size doesn't fit all. Sometimes people do start with passion, and that builds their talent. It's rare, but it happens. Sometimes they discover a talent but can't summon the passion to keep it going. Much of the time, they just need to make a living—and as they stick around and get good at their job, their passion often grows.

Society tends to celebrate the notion that if you're good at something, you should love it. But that's not always how it works. And people also like to say that if you love something, you are bound to become good at it. Not so. Sometimes it's enough just to love doing it, even if average is the best you'll ever be. No need to give it up, but you should probably find another way to make a living. If golf were how I made my living, I'd be living on the street.

We each must find our own way of fitting in. Some will find their calling early, while others will try many avenues—but I believe we each have our own road to success, even if it doesn't follow the script that society expects. Steve Jobs tried many things before he found that he had a natural talent for retail marketing.

There's no guarantee, but sometimes it happens: Passion and talent finally come together and line up like a perfect shot down the fairway that lands triumphantly on the green. You find not only that you are good at what you do but also that you love what you do—and when that happens, who cares which came first? You have found the sweet spot.

THOUGHTS:

WHEN ONE STANDS, WE ALL RISE

Lately, I've been thinking a lot about two days in my life—a time I stood up for what was right and a time I didn't. The first was when I was just back from Vietnam, the sound of artillery still in my head, hoping for something far better than what I'd just witnessed. The second was when I was in my mid-thirties with a family, two kids, and a house in the suburbs.

Today, in my seventies, reflecting on the man I was, I still regret the day I held my tongue. I knew better—but knowing better is never enough.

In 1971, finally back in the States, I was stationed briefly at Fort Riley, Kansas. I shared a room with three other men, one of them Black. We all went out to a bar one night. The Black soldier was quite good at pool, and at one point a young woman challenged him to a game. As they cued up, her boyfriend, another soldier in our barracks, exploded into a racist tirade.

Back at the barracks, he demanded that we all shun this man who was the "wrong color" to be hanging with his girl. "I don't want anyone talking to him. I want him shut out," he told us. Most of the men complied, for fear of getting shut out, too—this demand was coming from a guy they all considered cool. My two white roommates went along with the crowd.

About two days of this nonsense was all I could take. I called out my roommates on how they were treating a man who, a few days earlier, had been a friend. "You know he's a good guy," I said. "So what are you doing? Why are you letting some racist jerk tell you who you can talk to?" They listened—and quickly came around. The rest of the men in the barracks soon followed suit. Things went back to normal, or as normal as anything could be in those days.

And then there was that other scene, years later. I was a fairly successful businessman. Most folks would say I was living the good life. My friend Ralph and I were waiting at an airport restaurant in Fort Lauderdale for our flight home from a golf trip.

Nearby, a man and his family were waiting for a table. I presumed they were from the Caribbean Islands, judging by their accent, and they were clearly excited to be in America. As they waited to be seated, the man lifted his camcorder onto his shoulder to record their surroundings, as if to preserve the first day of their trip for all time.

I will always regret what happened next—or rather, what didn't happen. That family waited a long time for a table. Every time one opened, it went to a white customer. There was nothing subtle about the racism.

My friend and I just sat there. We both saw what was happening, but neither of us spoke up to challenge the hostess. One after another, she seated white families right away as they arrived, while ignoring the Black family. Eventually, the man asked her why this was so—and it didn't go well. Airport security finally came over and made sure the family got a table. Still, the damage was done. This was how America had welcomed that family.

Over the years, I have often thought about that episode at the airport. At the time, I was ashamed, embarrassed by my own inaction. All these years later, I still am. When we say nothing, we say plenty. My silence still screams at me.

Why, in my thirties, didn't I react the way I did fifteen years earlier? You would think I'd have grown more confident, not less, about my convictions. I knew better, yet I didn't do better. I've often wondered what changed me from the man who spoke up to the man who looked aside.

It's true I had more to lose than I did when I was younger. I was settling into midlife with its many responsibilities. I was comfortable. I was getting ahead. As a result, I had more skin in my pocket than skin in the game. I had something to protect—but what I most needed to protect was my sense of integrity and justice.

At times I feel as if I'm watching an old movie featuring a man named Bill Carr during different seasons of his life. Who is that young fellow, wearing Army green, demanding that his roommates stop snubbing a friend who had done nothing wrong? Who is that man in the polo shirt and chinos, biding time with a golf buddy as an injustice unfolds before their eyes? Who are those guys? They're me. It's all me.

I am aware that both those men still are within me, waiting to come out. It's not that I ever lacked compassion for what others endure. I can still summon that youthful sense of conviction and urgency. And I can still find reasons not to reach out. I am capable of both advocacy and indifference. We're all better off when we acknowledge the frailties of our humanity.

Hindsight gives us clarity. It's OK to regret moments from the past. And it's OK to be proud of your better moments. Our experiences matter because they shape us. We shouldn't dwell on the past, but we can't discount it, either. It is rich in lessons that will help us move forward.

I count myself fortunate for both those experiences. They remind me of who I want to be. In retrospect, they were both relatively minor matters in a world of appalling injustices. If I paused to think about it, there would be way too many to list. We would do well to pause and think more often.

There comes a time to say "Enough's enough." If you recognize one of those times but fail to respond, your conscience kicks in. I'm sure you have felt that ache of regret. Fighting injustice in its many forms is more than an individual responsibility. It's our collective responsibility. The measure of your personal success is how well you have helped others succeed. It's not about "what I have to lose." It's about "what we have to gain."

In my youth, I had the courage to act. I was true to myself, to my own core beliefs. I see now, more than ever, the importance of community. Whatever happens to our brothers and sisters happens to every one of us.

In the context of community, silence makes us complicit. If we consider ourselves part of the team, then we must also accept that looking the other way makes us part of the problem. Right or wrong, whatever each one of us does reflects on all of us. When we realize we are all in this together, "me" turns to "we."

THOUGHTS:

SECTION THREE

GIFTS YOU GIVE TO YOURSELF

What's it all about, this thing called life? Trying to figure it out, some people look in the rearview mirror, while others try to see around the turn ahead. Maybe you focus on achievement, or fame—or just on escaping the pain. Those things might come but can easily go. I have found that what makes life worthwhile is the here and now. Day by day, as we find our own way, the answers are within us. They are gifts we can give to ourselves.

In **"Breaking Away,"** I revisit a time when I stepped back from life's noise, giving myself several days to just go with the flow. We need times like that so we can recharge. Even a solitary walk, away from the chaos, can help us regain our footing. For some, it's a time of reflection. For others, it's a return to freedom.

"Reaching Out, Giving Back" is about helping others, even with small acts of kindness. When you take the focus off yourself, your own problems seem less pressing. You can see the wider world of people's needs and how you can make their lives a little better. By reaching out, we gain a deeper sense of purpose. When we serve others, we serve ourselves, too.

"The Power of Forgiveness" comes from freeing ourselves from the grip of resentment. Someone offends us, and we feel justified in returning the pain, either with burning words or the coldness of words left unspoken. Mostly, we hurt ourselves. When you forgive, you grow.

"Living in Gratitude" can transform how you experience life. Each of us can be thankful for the people who brighten our lives but whose efforts often go unnoticed. Who are the uncelebrated souls who gladden your heart? Have you told them?

"Showing the Way" is why we are here. Leadership is a serious responsibility, whether as a parent, a teacher, or a public servant. If we fail at this obligation, we fail one another. When you lead by example, inspiring and guiding others, you are giving a gift to them and to yourself.

"The Gift of Peace" comes from a life well-lived. We should all think now about the legacy we are leaving for others. Imagine hearing your own eulogy as loved ones gather for your funeral service. In this essay, you will learn about somebody who did.

BREAKING AWAY

After my divorce from my first wife, Sue, I grappled with so many questions. What could I have done differently? It's easy to rationalize. It's easy for people to say he or she did this or that, or said this or that—or "We just grew apart," whatever that might mean. Then the kids enter the fray, and they start questioning themselves. The blame game. Same old story.

Not for me. I was looking to put some blame on myself. Only by considering how it could be my fault would I be able to learn anything resembling a lesson out of the whole mess. I eventually concluded that I hadn't paid attention to what mattered to my wife. She was financially conservative and risk averse, and I wasn't. When the challenges came, I felt a bump in the road and adjusted the seat belt. She saw a head-on crash coming—understandably so, I suppose. Either way, I made decisions without minding her mindset, and so it was our marriage that crashed.

For years, since the early 1980s, Sue and I and our kids would often travel down to Sarasota, Florida. My boss had a place there, and he and I were friends—in fact, his kids and our kids were friends, too. Our families would hang out together on Thanksgiving holidays.

This time, I traveled there alone. I guess you could say I was still shell-shocked. Upon landing at the airport, that same old feeling came over me, stronger than ever: *These people here are way too slow!* I'm a born-and-bred Chicago boy. Sarasota is, well, different. Driving my rental car from the airport, I punched at the horn more than once. Yeah, I was pretty hyped-up.

Ordinarily, I try to plan my days and weeks hour by hour, convinced I must do it that way because otherwise I don't do it well. I compensate by ordering my steps in predictable ways, as if by habit. I'll get up in the morning at the same time. I'll go to the gym on the same days each week. Breakfast and dinner, right on schedule. A time and a place for my golf game.

In my Sarasota hotel room, I tossed my luggage on the bed, fumbled for a fresh shirt, and splashed water on my face at the sink. I squinted into the mirror. I looked too old for a still-young man. "You know what, fellow?" I told my reflection. "We're not planning a thing. We're not even going to *think* about anything. Nothing! We're just going to go with the flow and see what happens."

I looked around the room, then down at my suitcase, half-open on the edge of the bed. I noticed a battered paperback sticking out of a side pocket in the lining. I vaguely recalled picking it up on some previous trip, maybe from a bargain bin at an airport bookstore. I thumbed through it. It was a book on breathing exercises and meditation. So I gave it a try. Why not? I inhaled and exhaled a few times. I wrinkled my brow and started pondering stuff—because isn't that what you do when you meditate? I must have looked like the statue *The Thinker*. I had a lot to learn.

Feeling a twinge of hunger, I picked up the hotel's welcome folder and began looking at the lists of restaurants and nightlife—and then quickly remembered my pledge. No planning. No thinking. I would do whatever I felt like doing when I felt like doing it. I went for a walk along the beach. No destination in mind, no plans for dinner.

I passed a beachside bar and stopped for a beer. I smelled barbecue somewhere and followed my nose.

That's the way I spent my days. One afternoon, I drove down to Venice on a whim, found a barstool to occupy, and settled in to listen to a guy with a guitar and a great voice. What more could I want? I did notice a lot of golfer types in town. Turns out it was a Ladies Professional Golf Association event. I guess if I don't go looking for golf, golf comes looking for me.

I was in Sarasota for five days—and I watched myself decompress and de-stress. And you know what I found out? I didn't particularly like going to the gym, and I didn't like golf quite as much as I thought I did.

Change is hard to make and even harder to keep. Maybe you have seen the old movie *Charly*, starring Cliff Robertson. Charly has an IQ of 69 and can barely function in society. His coworkers torment him at the bakery where he works as a janitor. After a radical medical experiment, Charly acquires average intelligence, then progresses into genius territory. He falls in love with his tutor, but his emotional IQ can't catch up. As Charly and his tutor struggle with that conflict, Charly begins to regress. His newfound brilliance slips away. Easy come, not-so-easy go. It's hard to watch it happen—at least, it was for me.

During those five days in Florida, I felt a transformation as I decompressed from my "normal" life. I was slowing down. I discovered that the people around me weren't idiots after all. Feeling no obligation to choose one thing over another, I lived each moment as it came. I kept my mind free of the stray thoughts that typically bombarded me. I fended off all disturbances, whether from within or from without. It's not that they stopped coming at me, but when they did, I just quietly observed them, acknowledged them, and set them aside.

By week's end, I was no longer the hyped-up hot mess who had arrived at the airport. Soon, though, I was back at that airport, boarding a plane that would whisk me back to a place where leaning on the horn is a way of life. After landing at Chicago Midway Airport, I couldn't help noticing something: *These people here are nuts!* Loud and impatient, they ran in circles, getting onto planes and off, pushing to be first in line.

Welcome home? I felt as if I were returning from a different planetary system.

The next day, I looked up an old friend and told him my story. "I'm still feeling chill," I said, "but just wait and see. Watch what happens." I already knew, but I couldn't stop it. Back on my native soil, I regressed into hyperdrive. And I chose to do it. After days of going with the flow, I chose to flow right back into the daily stress. I couldn't just chuck my responsibilities as a dad and as a businessman. I was forty-one, with two kids, and recently divorced. I had a career to manage. I had bills to pay. Wasn't *hectic* part of the deal?

Still, I learned something important from those five days of freedom: the importance of breaking away. Your brain needs to clean out the clutter between the synapses. That's what it tries to do when you get a good night's sleep, too, but if you're like many people on the treadmill, a solid eight hours every night doesn't come easy. We all need to claim some time for ourselves.

Breaking away is a conscious decision to step back from obligations and expectations. It isn't about escaping or avoiding them, however. You aren't shirking your duties. Quite the opposite: You will deal all the better with them once you stop overthinking everything and are able to see your real priorities.

You're doing more than taking a break. You're taking control. After disengaging for a while, you can reconnect with a greater sense of purpose. All those daily details, as critical as they seem, no longer blind you to bigger pictures. You can better see whether the life you are leading is one you have chosen and that fulfills you, not just one you have drifted into.

After Sarasota, I realized I had more control over my life than I'd believed. Life could be different. I knew that if I took the time to clear my head, I could pay more attention to what mattered most, such as relationships and special moments. It's one thing to make it to your kid's soccer game; it's quite another to really be there.

To this day, whenever too much is hitting the fan, I will take a half-hour drive—no radio, no audiobooks—or a solitary stroll to nowhere in particular, and then just sit on a bench and feel myself breathing, free of the world's noise swirling in my head. If you've ever done that, you know what I mean.

The human brain thrives if we treat it well, and it suffers if we deny it the rest it needs. Sleep experts know this, as they measure eye movements and dream stages and such. Neuroscientists know it, too, as they watch their scanners reveal, in vivid color, how the brain reacts to their probes. Science has examined how mindful meditation can help us fight off disease and even influence the rate at which our cells age.

As for me, I know the value of breaking away because I have lived it. Whenever I turn off my thinking for a time and just let myself *be*, I feel cleansed. I can feel my brain getting rid of the junk it has absorbed, like dirt from a sponge. Try it. Find a bench and just sit. Gift yourself that gift.

THOUGHTS:

REACHING OUT, GIVING BACK

On Thanksgiving, my family forms a circle, hand in hand, wherever we may be—on the beach or at home or, as in our latest gathering, on a boat with dozens of others. This annual ritual keeps us grounded not only in gratitude but in what matters even more: reaching out to others. Giving back a portion of what has come our way. Putting gratitude into action.

As we stood near the boat together that Thanksgiving of 2023, I invited my stepdaughter Jessica and her husband, Kurt, to say a few words. They had recently welcomed their second child, Louie, after a long, challenging journey. They were grateful, they said, to have another little boy in their family. Smiling, they looked down at their firstborn, three-year-old Ollie.

"And what are you thankful for, Ollie?" his mom asked.

With eyes wide and bright, he blurted it out: "Doughnuts!"

We laughed. So did others nearby who happened to hear. Ollie's unbridled enthusiasm sent out a ripple of joy throughout the people around us. Kids are so silly, right?

It struck me, though, that what we do for others is often more about simple things than grand gestures. Gentle, unassuming kindnesses. A taste of life's small pleasures.

I smiled and looked around our circle. "You know, Christmas is coming, and here's an idea," I said. "Don't go buying me anything this time. Here's the gift I want from each of you. Sometime between now and then, give a dozen doughnuts to someone who wouldn't expect it—and if they ask why, don't explain. Just say, 'Because.'"

The idea was a hit. Soon, we were each sharing stories about small acts of kindness, given and received, sometimes anonymously but always without fanfare, without expectation. I thought perhaps these doughnut deliveries could become a family tradition for the holiday—our Ollie-day, you might say.

Sure, our grandson was just saying doughnuts are good. He didn't mean anything more profound than that. Still, if we keep it up, I'm sure he will grow to see that things just as sweet, even if only a smile or kind word, can multiply and diversify to become the catalyst for great change—or, as we put it that day, "the Ollie-fication of the world!"

Imagine if this caught on in a big way. Look around at the possibilities: Whose day might you brighten—that of a neighbor, or the crossing guard, or the office janitor you pass wordlessly by each day? Maybe someone who angered you so long ago you can't remember why. Or a total stranger. If you like others to appreciate you, try appreciating others—just because.

It's all in the spirit of reaching out to our fellow travelers on this planet: making connections, building relationships, serving others. That often takes more effort than a slap on the back or a quick stop at Dunkin', of course. Small kindnesses have a cumulative power, but they're not enough when the need is immediate and compelling, and ours is a world of so many needs.

To be generous with your time is a sound investment in all our futures. But where do you start? If you decide to serve others as a volunteer, how do you choose among so many prospects? The path isn't always clear.

My stepson Matt once asked me for some advice about that. I suggested that he look within. What experiences in his life had the most emotional impact on him? I knew he had recently lost a close friend to suicide and that the tragedy still weighed heavily on his heart.

My thoughts flashed back fifty years to the time my brother Kevin was severely injured in a motorcycle crash. I told Matt how my mom reacted: "She began thinking, *What can I do? How can I make this better*? She couldn't undo the accident, but she figured she could reach out to folks going through the same kind of thing." I explained that my mom had found her calling as one of the founders of what is now the Brain Injury Association of Illinois. She joined with four others whose loved ones had suffered traumatic head injuries, and they built an organization dedicated to working with doctors and hospitals to do everything possible for them. Her passion was born from pain, and through her service, she found meaning and purpose.

The passions that motivate are many. A carpenter picks up a guitar one day at a friend's house. He tries out a chord. Two hours later, he's still strumming. He's still a long way from appearing onstage, but he soon finds himself volunteering to build a stage at the local music festival. An emergency room physician fears she's burning out mid-career. She takes a sabbatical at a third-world clinic, caring for children. She remembers why she wanted to be a doctor—and back at the hospital, she feels a renewed energy and dedication for her work.

Whatever capacity you choose to serve in should reflect your core values. Often, this drive to help comes from a place of compassion or empathy. They're both from the heart—but there's a difference.

Compassion is easier. You are compassionate when you offer comfort to someone struggling. You acknowledge the pain, but you can keep it at arm's length. Empathy demands more. You experience the pain with them. You are in their shoes, committed to making a difference. When you tell a grieving friend you're just a phone call away, that's compassion. When you show up, sit with them, and share in their tears, that's empathy.

Empathy often comes from having shed such tears yourself. It drives you to act. You're not just observing. You're engaging. Empathy is what led to the founding of organizations such as Mothers Against Drunk Driving. It led to Sandy Hook Promise, through which parents who had lost their children in the Sandy Hook school shooting turned their grief into a mission against gun violence. Following the Parkland high school shooting, student survivors mobilized to lobby for changes to gun laws. The list goes on, tragedy after tragedy, as determined friends and loved ones try to bring some sense to what is senseless.

When the pain is severe and widespread, empathy can become a movement, such as the fights for civil rights, women's rights, and the freedom to love and marry whom you choose. All have been fueled by people who have lived the struggle and felt the injustice. They couldn't stand by as mere observers.

From wherever it springs, the spirit of generosity—the desire to give of one's time or resources—benefits both the receiver and the giver. Back in my college days after Vietnam, when money was tight, I gave my last $100 to a friend who was struggling to pay rent. My girlfriend thought I was nuts, but I knew we'd find a way to make it work. And we did. That act of giving didn't just help my friend; it was an expression of who I was and who I was becoming.

If you feel such a drive to serve others, you might wonder where it came from. For me, it might have started with my mom, who cared deeply for others. Maybe it was also instilled by all the other moms in the neighborhood, who took care of me after she passed. Perhaps it was growing in me during the late-night conversations I had with a buddy in a war zone as we stood watch and talked about all the people who never had a chance and how education could be the key to changing their lives.

As I reflect on my life and career, I see the patterns. Whatever I do, I feel compelled to do it well. And I feel, deep within, a responsibility to help others become their best, too, as they strive to find their way.

I think often of my seventh-grade math teacher, who reached out to me when I was struggling with algebra. My poor performance wasn't exactly surprising, since I wasn't keeping up with the reading nor doing much of my homework. I was getting the grades I deserved.

Nonetheless, she looked past my deficits and saw in me a potential untapped, if not yet emerging. Clearly, at that point, I wasn't striving to be my best. I wouldn't get to that point for years to come—really, not until after my time in the wilderness that was Vietnam, when I woke up to what could be.

Truth be told, I was embarrassed to need the help. But my teacher worked with me, patiently catching me up to the rest of the class. "Okay, we're fine now," she told me one day. "That's enough."

"No, it's not," I told her. "I don't just want to be even with everyone. I want to be ahead of them." This was my innate competitive streak speaking, in part, as well as a nagging fear that I might fall behind again and would need a buffer zone.

That extra help made all the difference. Math became my sweet spot, and I went on to take every science and math course I could in high school and then, in college, to pursue advanced degrees in chemistry. Who knew that a bit of extra help in seventh grade would set me on that path?

Though I decided, when close to my doctorate, that my future would not be as a chemistry professor, the spirit of generosity has remained with me always. I have tried to play that role in my family and with friends and colleagues. In fact, it became foundational to the mission of the IT company I eventually founded, where we are teammates, looking out for one another's best interests as we work to better all our lives.

My daughter Claire, even at age seven, understood what we were all about. One afternoon, while she was visiting me at the office, she showed me a list she had drawn, in crayon, to tape on my door. "This is for you, Dad," she said, and handed it to me. It was titled "Things You Need to Do to Work at York." First was: "Put in a good day's work." Next was: "Play nicely with others." And third: "You must have a good attitude." We had those words carved in wood, to hang prominently in both our Minneapolis and Chicago offices. To this day, they remind York's people of our responsibilities to one another.

As I have told my family, their job is to make the world a little bit better just by being in it. That could mean raising good children, participating in charitable activities, or simply being a good friend. Small gestures can create a ripple effect, inspiring people to likewise engage with others and with their communities.

As my father often said of his neighbors: "I take care of them, and they take care of me." Putting others first can lead to a fulfilling life. In my career, I have often reminded my colleagues of the need to build strong relationships and that they should do so in the spirit of mutual growth.

During interviews, my style was to always ask people about their backgrounds and upbringing. By knowing where they came from, I can better understand their values and motivation. Virtually everyone has a unique story worth exploring. I've encountered extraordinary individuals in my community, each with their own fascinating tales.

When you reach out and give back, when you hear people's stories and share in their struggles and victories, you are doing more than helping them. You are fostering the kind of connections that build communities. In service to others in need, you feel a swell of gratitude for what has come your way, and you want to do even more. You have given more than a gift to others. You are giving a gift to yourself.

You can start with the smile, the compliment, the token of appreciation. The bigger gestures can come later, in whatever way you might feel inclined. For now, plant that seed, and see what grows from it. You will enrich not only the lives of others but your own life as well. You can leave each day a little better than you found it.

Try it. It works. I bet you dollars to doughnuts you can make a difference.

THOUGHTS:

THE POWER OF FORGIVENESS

Forgiveness is a healer of wounds, a mender of broken souls—and for my younger brother Tom, it was a power that reshaped his life.

Tom's tale is one of resilience after a turbulent upbringing in our home on the South Side of Chicago. When our father remarried, we became a blended family of ten children—four boys and a girl on each side—but our parents weren't often present in that house. To ensure their marriage would survive, they spent a lot of time at their lake cottage instead.

By getting away for a time from the chaos of a houseful of teenagers, they hoped to demonstrate to us the importance of maintaining a loving relationship. They took with them our youngest brother, who was only nine and too young to be left with us.

At age twelve, Tom was the next youngest. My stepsister and I, both eighteen, soon departed for college, leaving him vulnerable to however his older brothers chose to treat him. As he would later describe it: "Shit rolls downhill, and I was at the bottom."

While still in high school, Tom felt he had to leave the house, and he never finished school. He joined the Navy but was promptly thrown out after only nineteen days. He lived in a friend's basement before finding a job as the manager of a slum rental building on the South Side of Chicago. It was seven stories with fifty-four units, one of which he lived in. He was only seventeen years old.

Tom's young life was filled with turmoil. He felt moments of despair and at times considered ending it all. I became familiar with the role of a caregiver, often finding myself on the other end of a phone call. I listened to Tom's agonized voice as he grappled with thoughts of self-harm and suicide. "It's not worth living," he would say. "I'm useless."

I remember going to look for him once and finding him in his basement apartment. Marijuana smoke billowed out at me when I opened the door. He was slumped in a chair, one of mine that I didn't know was missing. Blasting from the stereo was Pink Floyd's *The Wall.*

Despite his tumultuous circumstances, Tom possessed a remarkable ability to talk his way through situations. He did manage to get a few janitorial jobs, and he was a pretty good salesman, but he couldn't keep a job for long.

Then, about twenty-five years ago, Tom made a courageous decision. He would confront our father. He would tell him about the trauma he had endured. Tom took our father to see his therapist, preparing himself for a session filled with tears and anger. Instead, he said only this: "Dad, I didn't feel safe growing up."

Those simple words cut through years of pain and sorrow that had gone unspoken. In the hierarchy of human needs, security and love are foundational. Tom distilled his years of suffering into this core message: a plea for the safety that he felt he had been denied. Although our father's response was initially muted, something shifted. Following the session, Tom soon noticed that both our parents began telling him that they loved him, something he never remembered experiencing before.

Tom chose forgiveness. The moment he spoke those words marked the beginning of that journey. He knew forgiveness would be essential to his own healing, and it had to be his choice, not contingent upon anyone's apologies. He had to release the anger and resentment that had festered inside him for so long.

Tom forgave himself, as well. He came to see that you need to forgive others before you can forgive yourself; otherwise, you will be holding on to resentments. When you forgive others, there's nobody to blame anymore. No more excuses. The only person remaining to face is yourself.

Tom's journey of self-forgiveness took years. Once he had finally taken a look at himself, what he saw was a mess. He took stock of what needed to change in his life and began addressing those issues, one by one. I attended counseling sessions with him, and on one particularly distressing Easter, I took him to a mental institution. He admitted himself, hoping to find the peace that had eluded him for so long.

To further his healing, Tom channeled his creativity by writing a book titled *The Dog You Feed*. Writing it served as therapy for him; he was able to share his own struggles and aspirations. In his complex journey from darkness to light, the book's protagonist parallels Tom's life. It took him ten years to write the book, and in that time, he laid bare his past, his present, and his hopes for the future.

As time went on, Tom's life changed dramatically. He got a job as the maintenance manager for the Chicago International Produce Market. He bought a house and made major improvements to it. He quit smoking. No longer a troubled young man, Tom was maturing, achieving, growing. Continuing to explore his talents, he composed symphonies. He started to participate in his community. A garden he cultivated became part of the Blue Island garden walk.

Today, as I write this essay, my little brother Tom is sixty-eight years old and content with life. He swims, enjoys frequent walks around Lake Catherine, and cherishes simple pleasures. He calls me almost every day, radiating happiness in each conversation. His relationship with our parents became strong over the years. He calls our stepmom several times a week to catch up on life—and I'm sure they talk more than a little about God. Like me, Tom has doubted whether God exists, but he also tells me his slowly developing faith helped to carry him through the tough times. He's not unlike our dad, who began attending church later in life. Tom once asked him why. Dad responded, "I don't know, but it just works." He was a man of few words but infinite meaning.

Tom's decision to forgive others and himself was what finally broke his shackles of anger. It allowed him to move from trauma to contentment. He found healing, happiness, and hope. Tom's story demonstrates the enduring strength of the human spirit and the power of forgiveness. The examples are all around us—if we choose to look for them.

I vividly remember the day back in 2015 when I turned on the television to see President Barack Obama singing *Amazing Grace*. It was part of his eulogy at the funeral service for the pastor of Emanuel African Methodist Episcopal Church in Charleston, South Carolina, where a racist gunman killed nine people attending a Bible study.

I think about that amazing word, "grace." I am not a deeply religious man and didn't raise my family to know all about God, but I did raise them to know *Good*—and isn't that pretty much the same? President Obama was singing about goodness. *Amazing Grace* is a song of praise for the divine gift of grace, of mercy, of forgiveness.

At the killer's bond hearing, the judge invited the loved ones of the victims to say a few words, face-to-face with the perpetrator.

A woman who had lost her mother in the barrage of gunfire stood up and addressed him. "I forgive you," she said, "and have mercy on your soul." Her words resonated through the courtroom. Several other family members then stood to say the same. None of them had planned to do so. The outpouring of forgiveness came spontaneously.

The white supremacist gunman had hoped to start a race war. What happened was something far different. It was a powerful display of the human capacity to forgive even in the face of unimaginable tragedy. One person leading the charge can have a ripple effect, influencing not only those directly involved but also the millions of others who hear the story.

Pent-up anger can corrode the soul. How often have we heard "I could never forgive him!" as if forgiveness were a prize you can award? Forgiveness shouldn't depend on whether the other person deserves it. It's a gift we give ourselves. It's freedom from resentments. When we choose to forgive, we choose not to be imprisoned by the past—and that often requires forgiving ourselves, too.

We all have fallen short of our own expectations. Those memories can be painful. We may be tempted to let them linger as a constant reminder, like a scar. But to truly forgive yourself, you need to acknowledge your own faults and mistakes, learn from them, and move forward all the wiser. Not one of us is above it all. We will each make mistakes that hurt ourselves and others. The question then is what we will do about it.

In my own life, I have offended others. Though I didn't mean to hurt them, I believe in taking responsibility for my words and actions. Seeking forgiveness, I apologize sincerely, trying to mend the rift. Forgiveness becomes a way to repair and strengthen relationships. When anger subsides, fellowship grows.

Forgiveness shouldn't depend on getting an apology, however. You shouldn't withhold it until the other person shapes up to meet your standard. That might never happen, leaving you trapped in bitterness. It is never too late to forgive—even when the one who hurt you has been decades in the grave.

"Forgive and forget" is so easy to say, but forgiveness is not about forgetting. Some things I don't want to forget. I want to remember every detail, for example, of what my son went through with addiction. I was there for Jeff, but can I say the same for others who needed me? I want to recall the times when I failed to show up for people. If I forgive myself and forget, I fear I might do it again—and that is why I want to keep feeling those twinges of regret.

We can still regret our mistakes while holding on to the lessons learned and the empathy gained. Forgiveness allows us to carry the weight of those mistakes. They need not drag us down. Instead, what we learn from them can guide us into better days.

It took years, but my brother learned that forgiveness is compassion. It uplifts individuals, and it uplifts communities. It clears the wreckage of the past so the soul can heal. Forgiveness is an amazing grace.

THOUGHTS:

LIVING IN GRATITUDE

When I decided to name my senior partner, Richard Walker, as the new CEO of our company, I knew I had to give him the freedom to run it as he saw fit. I asked only that he not change our company's culture. "It's our secret sauce," I told him.

Richard knew this, of course, because he had been instrumental in building our culture, which looks out for the best interests of all our team members. And I reminded him of someone else at our company who embodied our culture, someone indispensable: Pat Jones.

Pat wasn't just a receptionist. She was the heart and soul of our company. For nearly thirty years, she greeted me and everyone else who walked through our doors with a sparkling smile. She didn't just do her job. Each day, she gave all of us a gift. Pat was an oasis of joy where we could feel refreshed even on the toughest of days.

"When the time comes that Pat retires," I told Richard, "I want to pay her the difference between her Social Security and what she makes now—you can just take it out of my own salary if necessary. I want her to come and go as she pleases." He of course agreed.

One morning, as once again Pat's buoyant spirit greeted me as I got off the elevator, I wondered whether anyone had ever thanked her—not just for working the front desk, but for the way she worked it, for her years of pleasantries, for being the special soul that she was.

So many times, even when we feel grateful for what others have done for us, we hold back on saying so, and they never know. Those folks could use a lift, too. I'm sure that Pat, for all her smiles, had her share of struggles.

At my desk, I took out pen and paper to jot down a note for her—and it soon became a letter.

As I searched for just the right words, I recognized how much Pat had influenced my life. I needed to express more than the kind of "thank you" that you say, almost by reflex, when somebody does you a favor. She had done us many small favors, indeed, but collectively they amounted to much more.

When I wrote that letter to Pat, something shifted inside me. I felt a deep sense of gratitude and recognized its power to shape our lives. It's a lot like love, in that it lives as a happy place in the heart. Simply acknowledging someone else's contribution to your life can fill you with a sense of joy and fulfillment. Though your intent is to brighten that person's day, you brighten your own day, too.

When we offer thanks, we generally recount the big things, like a loving family or a successful career. We tend not to recognize the everyday moments. They go unnoticed. In my letter to Pat, though, I let her know I'd been noticing for years. I concluded the letter like this: "You made my life better by being part of it. You and your Christian soul will always be with me."

Afterward, I got to thinking about others who had meant much to me in my life. I thought of Richard, who had become like a brother to me. He was not just a great salesperson. He was a great guy. In leading our company, he showed the same dedication and passion that have always defined him.

I have many letters I need to write—to my family, to old friends, and even to people I haven't spoken to in years. Gratitude should be a daily practice. We must not rush through life without pausing to appreciate the people we share it with and the moments we have shared together. With a heart of gratitude, life feels more fulfilling, less anxious.

As we express gratitude, we develop deeper relationships, both personal and professional. On the job, our colleagues feel appreciated. A strong workplace culture is the number one reason why people stay with a company, a *Harvard Business Review* study found. When employees like the people they work with, believe in the company's mission, and feel valued by their colleagues, they are more likely to be productive, motivated, and committed. I believe our company has thrived for so many years, and through hard times, because we have built a culture based on mutual respect and appreciation.

In my personal life, gratitude has deepened my relationships with family and friends. It's easy to get caught up in the demands of work and other responsibilities. Taking the time to show appreciation for the people who matter most has strengthened those bonds. Whether it's thanking my wife for her unwavering support or letting my children know how proud I am of them, these expressions of gratitude have brought us closer together.

Gratitude is more than just a feeling. It's a way of life. It's a dedication to looking for the good in any situation, as challenging as that can be. Even on the difficult days, there is always something to be thankful for. When you share that spirit with others, it spreads out in waves, like ripples on a pond.

The more we practice gratitude, the more it enriches us all. Just a few simple words can make someone's life a little better—and yours, too. Give it a try today, starting with two simple questions:

Who have been the most influential people in your life?

Have you told them?

THANK YOU, PAT JONES

This is the letter I wrote to Pat, our longtime receptionist, thanking her for being Pat:

Pat, you have been one of the most influential people in my life.

You may not know the following:

When my partner Julie and I sold our temporary-help business, the buyer got everything—all our clients and all our temporary help. Except for one. You.

Julie said they could have everything but Pat Jones. I said OK, but who is Pat Jones? She said you were the wonderful Black lady at our front desk who filled in when our receptionist was sick or on vacation.

I knew immediately who she was talking about because you always made me feel welcome when I got off the elevator.

I love coming to work every day ... well, almost every day. But for almost thirty years you have been there to greet me with your smile and your sweet words, "Hi there, Boss," or "Good morning, Boss," with uplifting energy in your voice.

On the days I would come in a little grungy, you wouldn't let me get by your desk without putting a smile on my face. I remember thinking, *I want to be in a bad mood, and now I can't.* ☺

You have been one of the most influential people in my life. For that, I say thanks. You made my life better for being part of it.

You and your Christian soul will always be with me.

—Bill, aka "Boss"

THOUGHTS:

SHOWING THE WAY

It was another busy morning at the airport. Passing through security, I noticed the trays were piling up at the end of the conveyor belt. Nobody seemed to care about the growing mess. They just wanted to get through the checkpoint as quickly as possible. Something compelled me to step forward. I took a moment to stack the trays, one on top of the other, then returned to my place in line.

What happened next surprised me. The next person behind me picked up his tray and neatly stacked it with mine. Then, one by one, the others stacked theirs, too. My gesture had changed the behavior of my fellow travelers. As I reflected on this, I realized that, while my action had set an example, it wasn't until the guy behind me decided to do the same as me that the group behavior changed. Though I had been the first to take action, it was the first follower who made it a trend.

During my frequent travels, I often manage to find a golf course, and I observed the same kind of behavior one peaceful morning at a practice green. As I chipped away, I saw that the green was littered with balls that earlier golfers had left scattered. After finishing my practice, I grabbed the ball sweeper and cleared them away. As I lingered, I noticed that the next golfer, who had been watching me, did the same when he was done, clearing the green after his practice.

Here again, I had done something simple that became an example for others to follow.

These stories illustrate a fundamental truth about leadership: The first person to act is often not the one who initiates change. In each of those cases, it was the first follower who set the expectation that others should do the same. The first to act shows the possibilities. The first follower shows the way.

In both instances, what I was experiencing was a trait of human behavior that, on a much larger scale, has influenced our course for countless generations. History is filled with examples of how the first followers can propel a movement.

Consider the fall of the Berlin Wall in 1989. A border guard, faced with a growing crowd, decided to open the gate—and that's when the movement took off. Other guards along the wall quickly followed his example. Thousands of people poured through, leading to the eventual collapse of the wall. It wasn't the first guard who made it all happen. And the first protestors didn't tear down that wall. History was in the hands of the followers.

Who can forget, that same year, the image of a lone protester standing in front of a column of tanks in Tiananmen Square? After he took his defiant stand, a group of people rushed out to him, pulling him away before the tanks could crush him. They saved his life—and accelerated a pro-democracy movement that it took China's military might to quell.

So many others. Rosa Parks's refusal to give up her seat on a segregated bus might have been an isolated act of defiance, but the following outcry turned her solitary stand into a key event in the Civil Rights Movement. The Stonewall uprising in Greenwich Village might have been just another police raid were it not for those who fought to turn the initial resistance into a national movement for gay rights. The Boston Tea Party, same idea. You get the picture. Somebody takes a stand, and others run with it. The momentum builds. A movement begins.

Movements can be good or bad, of course. It all depends on the character of those who step forward as the leaders. To effectively lead, you must have strong values of honesty, fairness, and commitment to others.

David Brooks, in his book *The Road to Character*, contrasts two types of virtues: "résumé virtues," which focus on career success and external achievements, and "eulogy virtues," which define our moral core and inner character—traits extolled at a funeral. He argues that true leadership and a lasting impact are built on these deeper eulogy virtues. We get them by overcoming personal weaknesses and developing qualities like kindness, humility, and bravery. Those are what endure.

Leading by example means not asking others to do what you haven't done or wouldn't do yourself. As the leader of my business, I made that clear to my colleagues. It's also a principle often seen in the military, where leaders are expected to endure the same hardships as their soldiers. That willingness communicates integrity, trust, and respect.

Leadership also requires consistency. People are quick to see through empty promises. They view half-hearted efforts with disdain. Consistency in your actions builds credibility and trust. If you fail to follow through on your words and commitments, you lose respect. You breed uncertainty and distrust, which results in disengagement and low morale. Your followers don't know what to expect from you. They will wonder if your words carry any weight.

The consequences can be disastrous. What happens, for example, if a CEO promises their company's employees yearly performance bonuses but consistently fails to deliver? The employees eventually become disillusioned. Productivity drops. Skilled workers leave. The company's reputation may suffer as the public's trust fades away.

Ultimately, leaders are measured by their influence on others. You don't gain influence through coercion or manipulation. You get it from leading by example. To be a good example to others, be a good example to yourself. Live according to your values. Maintain your integrity. If you do what's right for your own sake, you will inspire others to do the same.

Leading by example is the approach I have tried to take with my children and with my teammates at work. I've never thought of myself as having won or lost. I judge myself only by how I conducted myself. Was I a good example? Did I try my best? That's what counts in sports, and it counts in whatever serious endeavor you take on in life.

I am not outgoing by nature. I've often felt unsure of my footing in a crowd. Leadership has been a journey for me. Yet somehow, I always found myself in leadership roles, in my high school fraternity days, through college, and into my career. Leadership seemed to find me, even when I wasn't looking for it.

I have learned that being the loudest voice or the most charismatic person in the room doesn't make you a leader. What matters is how well you can build relationships, with persistence and caring. For whatever reason, I've always been able to figure out how to get people to work with me. They don't work *for* me; if anything, I work for them. I usually get to where I want to go, not through force but by persevering and finding a way to make things work. My job is to create an environment, a culture, where people want to be and where we work together as a team. I've never considered myself any more important than anyone else on the team.

Leadership isn't about grand gestures. It doesn't come from dramatic speeches. It comes from consistent actions that inspire others to follow. It comes from being there for them. A leader may be first to step forward, yes, but they must also be willing to be the first to follow, to stand side by side with their colleagues. It's hard to lead from a distant hill. To show the way, you must show up.

The principle of leading by example extends to my family life as well. My stepmom was clear that her marriage to our dad had to come first. I've carried that lesson into my own marriage, telling the same to my wife Breeda. The most important thing that parents can do for their children is to set an example of a good, loving marriage. That's a legacy that Breeda and I want to leave with our kids.

Navigating relationships within the family has required me to lead by example in ways that I hadn't expected. When I asked Breeda to marry me after knowing her only eight months, my children were naturally protective of me. For fifteen years, they had been my main focus. I made it clear that they now needed to establish their own relationships with Breeda outside of me—and they did.

One afternoon several years ago, during a family dinner that I cooked for us all, I excused myself to get something from the kitchen. At the doorway, I paused to look back at the table. I took note of who was talking to whom. I listened to the laughter. I smiled as I observed the web of connections that had formed among us. These bonds had grown strong—and not so much through the grand gestures as through the smiles, the tears, the countless moments of caring.

And there, with our family around her, was Breeda, the woman who had helped me become a better man. This was it. This was our legacy. This was how I wanted us to be remembered: as good people who had tried to live out their values, showing what mattered most to those who mattered most to them. If we have attained success, let it be by that measure.

THOUGHTS:

THE GIFT OF PEACE

You know you have found peace when you write your own eulogy while you still have a lot of game. I wrote mine probably twenty years ago. It was late one night, and I was thinking about how happy I'd been in life.

I'm not saying life has been easy since then or that I have all the answers. Far from it. Since I wrote my eulogy, my business has been through several tough times. Twice, I've had to move out of my house and rent it to someone else because I couldn't afford to live there. I sold my family cottage. I had to borrow several hundred thousand dollars for my business—and I was newly married. Not exactly a good start.

But we survived, and we still are.

I knew I could deal with it. There was a calmness in my karma. I never got angry, never got sad nor felt sorry for myself. Never blamed anyone or anything. I was focused, for sure, but not frantic.

Some call it being in the zone. I call it being at peace with yourself. Isn't that what it's all about? I knew shit happened in life. I knew life was not a straight line. I also knew it was my life, and the problems were mine to deal with—and that's OK. Remember, it's challenges that lead to growth.

I'm good if I go tomorrow. I've had a great life filled with happiness, sadness, success, and failure. I have a family I love dearly. Many good friends, some since high school. I've been broke, and I've had money—

it never mattered. As I like to say, I've had bad things happen to me, but I've never had a bad day (except when I've had the flu. That really sucks).

Write your own eulogy now. Why let someone else tell your story after you're gone? Tell it yourself, while you can. You could be gone tomorrow. As time goes on, you can always revise and update—but there's no better time than now to reflect on the good, the bad, the ugly. As you think back through your life, you gain the benefit of perspective—and my guess is you will see things differently from how you once did.

You may have heard how Alfred Nobel gained a new perspective. The Swedish chemist invented dynamite, initially used for mining but quickly put to military use. Nobel, whose family owned a factory that made cannons, said his invention held such power for mass destruction that it would make warfare unthinkable. Twenty years later, he sat down one morning with his newspaper and read that Alfred Nobel, "the merchant of death," was dead. He "became rich by finding ways to kill more people faster than ever before." It was Nobel's brother who had died. A reporter had confused the names.

In shock, Nobel examined his life. *Will this be my eulogy? Is this my legacy?* He decided to take control of his narrative. He rewrote his will and bequeathed his wealth to the establishment of the Nobel prizes for those who advance peace and the progress of humanity.

Think about it. How do you want to remember yourself, and how do you want others to remember you? If you write your own eulogy now and don't like what you see, you will likely still have time. You still have a chance to become who you want to be.

A few years after I wrote my eulogy, I fell in love with a beautiful woman named Breeda after being single for fifteen years. You probably wonder how this relates. Hang with me.

Breeda's son Anthony was in Los Angeles and worked for a small production company that did pilots, hoping for one to get picked up as a reality TV series. One such pilot was titled *The Funeral.* It was about a woman planning her funeral—picking out her grave site, a coffin, flowers, and all the other details.

The person planning her own funeral … was my new girlfriend. Breeda's son had asked her to be the subject of the pilot episode, and she had agreed. She was sequestered. No one, including me, could have any contact with her for a week. Did I mention we had just started dating?

The cameras followed her around as she planned every aspect of her funeral—and even when she retreated to her bedroom. She cried, felt conflicted, felt alone. They broke her down. A lot of the emotions you see on reality TV shows are real.

After the initial filming, the funeral service was held in a beautiful woodland park. In attendance were it seemed like well over a hundred invited guests. Yes, they knew she was alive, but it didn't really matter.

As part of the ceremony, two people were chosen to speak about her life. Her best friend and (drumroll, you guessed it) me. I think I spoke eloquently about her and her life, considering I had known her for all of five months. *Who is this guy?* most people in the audience must have wondered.

Breeda was in a trailer watching the entire proceedings. All were invited to a "celebration of life" with Irish dancing and a good amount of alcohol. About halfway through the celebration, as the camera was still rolling, she came out from the shadows of death and, to the amazement of everyone, joined us in celebration. She did her first dance with her son the producer, and the second dance with me—and again, I could tell what people were thinking: *Who is this guy?*

I can only imagine how Breeda felt as she watched from the trailer as people spoke about who she was and what she meant to them. She got to hear others deliver her eulogy. If she had written her own, I've often wondered, how might it have compared?

That all happened just a few years after I'd written my own eulogy, and I took another hard look at the words I had put down. Was I living a life I would be proud of? What should come next? Those are the kind of questions that such an exercise forces you to ask yourself.

And here are two more: Do you like yourself? Do you respect yourself? Maybe you were born in the wrong zip code. Maybe your parents were not good examples. But as science has shown many times, your brain has "plasticity." This means whatever you think of yourself now can be changed. This is the true gift of life. No matter what has happened, you can overcome it by rewiring your brain.

Sound weird? It is actually simple. You can choose your own inputs. You can choose what to read, listen to, and watch. You can decide who you hang with. You can be a person you like and respect.

It won't happen overnight. It took decades for you to become who you are. The good news is your new choices will wire your brain so you can become the person you want to be much faster than you think. You will notice some changes in a matter of weeks.

I didn't write my own eulogy because I was expecting to die. I did it because I expected to live, and to live more fully. I did it to take stock of my life and find peace. As grateful as I was about my life, there were still "holes" to fix. As you write your own eulogy, odds are you'll find some holes of your own, and there's no better time to start patching them than right now.

Who is this guy? I, too, am trying to figure that out. Every day, in my pursuit of peace, I discover new things about myself. Just as forgiveness and gratitude are gifts you give yourself, so too is peace. No one else needs to do anything for you to experience it. It comes from knowing who you are and knowing who you want to be—and the closer those two things are to each other, the more peace you will have.

THOUGHTS:

PARTING THOUGHTS

WE'RE IN THIS TOGETHER

Thank you for coming along with me for a while. I didn't intend this book to be simply a collection of my own stories—although, granted, I've packed in plenty of them. I wrote these essays at various times through the years as I was making my way through life. If I did what I set out to do by collecting them into a book, you have spent a lot of time thinking and reflecting on your own stories.

My journey hasn't been all that special. What's special are the themes of life we share. Your stories have different characters than mine. The plot is altogether different. But as the years pass and our hair turns gray, we come to see that no matter where we roam, others have walked that path.

As we've often heard, there's nothing new under the sun—and isn't there something weirdly comforting about that? You feel a little less alone when you realize most people have felt or experienced something like what you're going through. It's just the details that change.

I wish I had asked my dad, before he passed, to tell me more of his stories. I wish we had compared notes about our lives. That's one of my biggest regrets. I wonder if he came to some of the same conclusions as I have.

Namely, this: Life has no guarantees. It is a crapshoot. We are born into a world that sometimes kicks us down and at other times raises us high, seemingly at random. We have no say on where or when we're born, or whether we're born at all. We set out on a road that sometimes seems so lonely—until we look around and see others with the same questions, struggles, and dreams. Though we have little control over much of what happens to us, we can always choose how to respond.

I designed this book to make each "chapter" an essay that can stand alone, available for a quick read. You could open it anywhere, and each essay would make sense, independent of the others. I did, however, arrange them in a sequence that reflects the three prevailing themes you encountered.

First, we explored how life is arbitrary, not a straight line. Then we considered how life is what we make of it as we each find our own way. And once we do, the rewards can be bountiful. Our relationships flourish. We feel a sense of penetrating peace.

Turns out we need not be at the mercy of life's randomness. We humans are a species blessed with resilience, if only we can find it. To be resilient doesn't mean you can avoid the storms. It means you can get through them. You can find your footing again to head on down that road—and make some meaningful relationships along the way.

As you have read these essays, no matter where you began, I hope you saw that power of resilience shining through. If life gives you a zig when you wanted a zag, you can learn to go with the flow. If you fall, you can rise. If others disappoint you—and they will—you can forgive them. You can forgive yourself, too.

Since we can't be sure where the road leads, why worry about where and when it ends? You can try to buy time with diets and pills and surgeries—but making life longer only makes sense if it also means living better. Our time on this planet shouldn't be treated like some countdown to the grave. What matters isn't the years of life we have, but rather the life we put into those years.

A long life without connection and fulfillment is no life at all. If you strive for wealth, do so knowing that what truly makes you rich is the quality of your relationships. How well did you love others—even those who seemed unlovable? How will you be remembered? Were you good to your word? Did you look out for other people's best interests? Those are the kind of questions that will define your legacy. You will have a trust fund like no other.

We're in this together, folks. Each day we can learn something new. Each day we can grow a little more. As we do, we are giving gifts to ourselves—the spirit of gratitude, for example, and of forgiveness, and so much more. Once we have found these treasures in ourselves, we can show the way to others. By sharing our stories, we bring the past into the present—and that will help us shape our future.

Rest assured, you can make it. By accepting what you can't control and focusing on what you can, you discover the gift of peace. It comes when you stop blaming the past and fearing the future. It comes when you learn to appreciate the present, knowing you have done your best with whatever came your way.

Now, as you step back into your own story, look around. What can you control? What can you let go? What can you do or say to make this day a little better for yourself and others? Remember, you can't rewrite the past, and you can't forecast the future, but day by day, you can choose how you want to live as you head forward. So buckle up—and enjoy the ride!

THOUGHTS:

BOOKS ON MY SHELF

Here are the books I have mentioned on these pages, plus a few others that I recommend. I have found a lot of wisdom in what these authors have to say, and I am confident that you, too, will appreciate their value.

Brooks, David. *The Road to Character.* Random House, 2015.

Buford, Bob. *Halftime: Moving from Success to Significance.* Zondervan, 1994.

Carr, Thomas Freeman. *The Dog You Feed: A Dark Journey Into Revenge.* Outskirts Press, 2011.

Clear, James. *Atomic Habits: An Easy and Proven Way to Build Good Habits and Break Bad Ones.* Avery, 2018.

Dweck, Carol S. *Mindset: The New Psychology of Success.* Random House, 2006.

Galloway, Scott. *Adrift: America in 100 Charts.* Portfolio, 2022.

Galloway, Scott. *The Algebra of Wealth: A Simple Formula for Financial Security.* Portfolio, 2024.

Grant, Adam. *Hidden Potential: The Science of Achieving Greater Things.* Viking, 2023.

Hill, Napoleon. *Think and Grow Rich: The Landmark Bestseller Now Revised and Updated for the 21st Century*. Revised and expanded by Arthur R.

Pell. Jeremy P. Tarcher/Penguin, 2005. Originally published in 1937 by The Ralston Society.

Kahneman, Daniel. *Thinking, Fast and Slow.* Farrar, Straus, and Giroux, 2011.

Kahneman, Daniel, Olivier Sibony, and Cass R. Sunstein. *Noise: A Flaw in Human Judgment.* Little, Brown Spark, 2021.

Maxwell, John C. *The 5 Levels of Leadership: Proven Steps to Maximize Your Potential.* Center Street, 2011.

McRaven, William H. *Make Your Bed: Little Things That Can Change Your Life ... And Maybe the World.* Grand Central Publishing, 2017.

Mullainathan, Sendhil, and Eldar Shafir. *Scarcity: Why Having Too Little Means So Much.* Times Books, 2013.

Nichols, Morgan Harper. *Peace Is a Practice: An Invitation to Breathe Deep and Find a New Rhythm for Life.* Zondervan, 2022.

Schuller, Robert H. *Tough Times Never Last, but Tough People Do!* Bantam Books, 1984.

Shetty, Jay. *Think Like a Monk: Train Your Mind for Peace and Purpose Every Day.* Simon & Schuster, 2020.

Sinek, Simon. *Leaders Eat Last: Why Some Teams Pull Together and Others Don't.* Portfolio, 2014.

Taleb, Nassim Nicholas. *Antifragile: Things That Gain from Disorder.* Random House, 2012.

Thaler, Richard H., and Cass R. Sunstein. *Nudge: Improving Decisions About Health, Wealth, and Happiness.* Yale University Press, 2008.

Vanderkam, Laura. *168 Hours: You Have More Time Than You Think.* Portfolio, 2010.

Walker, Richard. *Relationship Equity: Your Cornerstone Investment to Great Gains in Business and Life.* Forbes Books, 2023.

Young, Sarah. *Jesus Calling: Enjoying Peace in His Presence.* Thomas Nelson, 2004.